AGING ISSUES, HEALTH AND FINANCIAL ALTERNATIVE

MONEY MANAGEMENT FOR FINANCIAL CAREGIVERS

GUIDANCE AND RESPONSIBILITIES

AGING ISSUES, HEALTH AND FINANCIAL ALTERNATIVE

Additional books in this series can be found on Nova's website under the Series tab.

Additional E-books in this series can be found on Nova's website under the E-book tab.

AGING ISSUES, HEALTH AND FINANCIAL ALTERNATIVE

MONEY MANAGEMENT FOR FINANCIAL CAREGIVERS

GUIDANCE AND RESPONSIBILITIES

OLIVIA CROWDER
EDITOR

NOVINKA
New York

For permission to use material from this book please contact us:
Telephone 631-231-7269; Fax 631-231-8175
Web Site: http://www.novapublishers.com

Library of Congress Cataloging-in-Publication Data

ISBN: 978-1-63117-042-3

Published by Nova Science Publishers, Inc. † New York

CONTENTS

PREFACE

Managing money or property for a loved one who is unable to pay bills or make financial decisions can sometimes be overwhelming. But, it can also be a great opportunity to help someone you care about, and protect them from scams and fraud.

These chapters are meant to help financial caregivers. The *Managing Someone Else's Money* guides are for agents under powers of attorney, court-appointed guardians, trustees, and government fiduciaries (Social Security representative payees and VA fiduciaries.)

The guides help you to be a financial caregiver in three ways:

- They walk you through your duties.
- They tell you how to watch out for scams and financial exploitation, and what to do if your loved one is a victim.

They tell you where you can go for help.

In: Money Management for Financial Caregivers ISBN: 978-1-63117-042-3
Editor: Olivia Crowder

Chapter 1

MANAGING SOMEONE ELSE'S MONEY: HELP FOR AGENTS UNDER A POWER OF ATTORNEY[*]

American Bar Association Commission on Law and Aging

ABOUT THE CONSUMER FINANCIAL PROTECTION BUREAU

The Consumer Financial Protection Bureau, or the CFPB, is focused on making markets for consumer financial products and services work for families — whether they are applying for a mortgage, choosing among credit cards, or using any number of other consumer financial products. We empower consumers to take more control over their financial lives.

The CFPB Office for Older Americans is the only federal office dedicated to the financial health of Americans age 62 and over. Along with other agencies, the Office works to support sound financial decision-making and to prevent financial exploitation of older adults. To help people (including family members) with legal authority to handle an older person's money, the Office contracted and worked closely with the American Bar Association

[*] This guide was developed under contract for the Consumer Financial Protection Bureau and released October 2013.

Commission on Law and Aging to prepare this guide. Though the guide was developed by the American Bar Association Commission, it is not intended to provide legal advice or serve as a substitute for your own legal counsel. If you have questions or concerns, we recommend that you seek the guidance of the appropriate legal professional.

WHY READ THIS GUIDE?

Like many people, you may never have been an agent under a power of attorney before. That's why we created *Managing someone else's money: Help for agents under a power of attorney.* This guide will help you understand what you can and cannot do in your role as an *agent~* In that role, you are a *fiduciary*. For this guide, a fiduciary is anyone named to manage money or property for someone else. You'll find brief tips to help you avoid problems and resources for finding more information.

This guide is for family and friends serving as an agent, not for professionals or organizations. The guide does not give you legal advice. State laws vary, so you may have additional duties. Talk to a lawyer if you have questions about your duties.

If you want to learn about making a power of attorney, this guide is not designed for you. Talk to a lawyer or read other guides about powers of attorney from your state bar association or others.

LET'S START WITH A SCENARIO ABOUT HOW YOU MIGHT HAVE BECOME AN AGENT UNDER POWER OF ATTORNEY

Your family member or friend is worried that she will get sick and will not be able to pay her bills or make other decisions about her savings and her house. For this guide, let's call her Martina. Martina has signed a legal document called a *power of attorney*. In it, she names you as her agent and gives you the power to make decisions about money and property for her.

The law gives you a lot of responsibility as Martina's agent under a power of attorney.

You are now a *fiduciary* with *fiduciary duties*.

What Is a Fiduciary?

Since you have been named to manage money or property for someone else, you are *a fiduciary.* The law requires you to manage Martina's money and property for her benefit, not yours. It does not matter if you are managing a lot of money or a little. It does not matter if you are a family member or not.

The role of a fiduciary carries with it legal responsibilities. When you act as a fiduciary for Martina, you have four basic duties that you must keep in mind:

1. Act only in Martina's best interest.
2. Manage Martina's money and property carefully.
3. Keep Martina's money and property separate from yours.
4. Keep good records.

As a fiduciary, you must be trustworthy, honest, and act in good faith. If you do not meet these standards, you could be removed as a fiduciary, sued, or have to repay money. It is even possible that the police or sheriff could investigate you and you could go to jail. *That's why it's always important to remember: It's not your money!*

Power of Attorney Questions and Answers

What Is a Power of Attorney?

A power of attorney is a legal document. Martina made a power of attorney to give you legal authority to make decisions about her money or property so that you can make decisions for her if she is sick or injured. In some states, the type of document that Martina made is called a durable power of attorney.

Under a power of attorney, Martina is called the principal.

You are called the agent. Another name for the agent is attorney-in-fact.

Martina could also make a health care power of attorney if she names someone to make decisions about her health care. (We don't discuss a health care power of attorney in this guide, but if you want more information about that, go to www.ambar.org/healthdecisions.)

Different Types of Fiduciaries Exist

In your role as agent, you may act as or deal with other types of fiduciaries.

These may include:

Trustees under a revocable living trust—someone names them to manage money and property.

Representative payees or, for veterans, VA fiduciaries—a government agency names them to manage government money that is paid to someone.

Guardians or conservators—a court names them to manage money and property for someone who needs help.

Can Martina Still Manage Her Money and Property After Signing a Power of Attorney?

Yes, as long as she is still able to make decisions.

Can a Power of Attorney Be Changed or Revoked?

Martina can take away (or *revoke*) your authority to act as her agent at any time if she wants to and is still able to make decisions. If she does take away your authority as her agent, you must stop making decisions for her. Martina should tell any people or businesses you were dealing with about her decision to take away your authority.

What If You Think the Change Was the Result of Fraud or Abuse?

If you think Martina does not understand the decision she made to remove your authority and is being abused or exploited by someone else, talk to a trusted family member; a lawyer; or an official from adult protective services, the police, or the sheriff.

When Do Your Responsibilities End?

If Martina revokes your authority, your responsibilities end. In addition, your authority ends when she dies. Promptly notify her bank or other businesses with which you interacted as her agent. Even if you can easily pay some of her outstanding bills, you will no longer have the authority to do so. If you are married to Martina, your authority to act as her agent may end if you get divorced or legally separated. If a court names a guardian of property or conservator to act for her, your authority as agent may end. The power of attorney document or state laws govern these situations.

What Happens if You Can No Longer Serve as Agent?

If you are not able to act as Martina's agent and she cannot name someone else to act for her, tell a trusted family member or a government agency such as adult protective services. If you cannot act as her fiduciary, she will need someone else to help her.

Don't Expect Others to Know What an Agent Is or Does

They may not understand that you have been named as an agent. They may think that you have more authority or less authority than you really have. You may need to educate them. You could show them this guide.

FOUR BASIC DUTIES OF A FIDUCIARY

Duty 1. Act Only in Martina's Best Interest

Because you are dealing with Martina's money and property, your duty is to make decisions that are best for her. This means you must ignore your own interests and needs, or the interests and needs of other people.

To help act in Martina's best interest, follow these guidelines:

- *Read the power of attorney and do what it says.* Your authority is strictly limited to what the document and state law allow. Follow

Martina's directions in the document, even if you have the best intentions in doing something different.

- *Understand when the power of attorney becomes effective.* It may be right away or only when Martina can no longer make her own decisions. Check to see if the document says how you will know when Martina can no longer make her own decisions.
- *As much as possible, involve Martina in decisions.* Many things can affect your decisions about Martina's money and property. For example, you might feel pressure from others. Martina's abilities to make decisions might change from time to time.

Even after it is clear that you must make decisions for Martina, ask her what she wants if she can communicate. If she can't say what she wants, try to find out what she would have wanted. Look at any past decisions, actions, and statements. Ask people who care about Martina what they think she would have wanted. Make the decisions you think Martina would have wanted, unless doing so would harm her. Put her well-being above saving money for others who may inherit her money and property. Make sure she is safe and comfortable, and her needs are met.

- Avoid conflicts of interest. A conflict of interest happens if you make a decision about Martina's property that may benefit someone else at Martina's expense. As a fiduciary, you have a strict duty to avoid conflicts of interest—or even the appearance of a conflict of interest.
- Don't borrow, loan, or give Martina's money to yourself or others~ Even if the power of attorney or state law clearly allows gifts to you or others, be very careful to avoid conflicts of interest. Make sure that any gifts do not increase or complicate Martina's taxes or change her plans to give away her property when she dies. Any gifts or loans should be in line with what Martina would have wanted. For example, if Martina gave money every year to a charity, the power of attorney may allow you to continue doing that.
- Avoid changing Martina's plans for giving away her money or property when she dies. There may be rare situations in which changing Martina's plans would be in her best interest. But you should get legal advice to make sure that the power of attorney or state law allows that.
- Don't pay yourself for the time you spend acting as Martina's agent, unless the power of attorney or state law allows it. If you are allowed

to pay yourself, you need to show that your fee is reasonable. Carefully document how much time you spend and what you do.

Avoid Possible Conflicts of Interest

Sometimes people have good intentions, but do things they shouldn't. Because you are now a fiduciary, you should avoid any conflicts of interest. Here are a few examples of possible conflicts of interest:

Whose Car Is It?

You used Martina's money to buy a car. You use it to drive her to appointments, but most of the time you drive the car just for your own needs. This may be a conflict of interest.

Should You Do Business with Family?

Martina needs repair work in her apartment. You hire your son and pay him from Martina's money. This may be a conflict of interest, even though the work was needed. It appears that you have put your personal interest to benefit your son in conflict with Martina's interests.

Duty 2. Manage Martina's Money and Property Carefully

As Martina's agent, you might pay bills, oversee bank accounts, and pay for things she needs. You might also make investments, pay taxes, collect rent or unpaid debts, get insurance if needed, and do other things written in the power of attorney.

You have a duty to manage Martina's money and property very carefully. Use good judgment and common sense. As a fiduciary, you must be even more careful with Martina's money than you might be with your own!

Follow these guidelines to help you make careful decisions:

- *List Martina's money, property, and debts*. To make careful decisions, you need to know what Martina owns and owes. Your list might include:
  - Checking and savings accounts;
  - Cash;

- Pension, retirement, annuity, rental, public benefit, or other income;
- Real estate;
- Cars and other vehicles;
- Insurance policies;
- Trusts for which Martina is a beneficiary;
- Stocks and bonds;
- Jewelry, furniture, and any other items of value; and
- Unpaid credit card bills and other outstanding loans.

- Protect Martina's property. Keep her money and property safe. You may need to put valuable items in safe deposit boxes, change locks on property, and make sure her home or other property is insured. Make sure bank accounts earn interest if possible and have low or no fees. Review bank and other financial statements promptly. If Martina owns any real estate, keep it in good condition.
- Invest carefully. If you are making investment decisions for Martina, talk to a financial professional. The Securities and Exchange Commission (SEC) provides tips on choosing a financial professional at www.sec.gov/investor/alerts/ib_top_tips.pdf. Discuss choices and goals for investing based on Martina's needs and values.
- Pay bills and taxes on time.
- Cancel any insurance policies that Martina does not need.
- Collect debts. Find out if anyone owes Martina money, and try to collect it.
- Take steps to have the power of attorney accepted. Sometimes banks or other businesses won't do what you, acting as Martina's agent, want them to do. A bank may refuse to accept the power of attorney and want Martina to sign its own form. This is a problem if Martina has lost the ability to act for herself. As soon as you need to act as Martina's agent, contact any businesses (such as banks) or people that she deals with and give them copies of the power of attorney. Never give away the original document. You can get certified copies of the original document. If someone will not accept your authority as agent, talk to a supervisor. If they still won't accept it, talk to a lawyer. State law may require the business or person to accept the power of attorney.

Can Martina Get Any Benefits?

Find out if Martina is eligible for any financial or health care benefits from an employer or a government. These benefits might include pensions, disability, Social Security, Medicare, Medicaid, Veterans benefits, housing assistance, or food stamps (now known as Supplemental Nutrition Assistance Program or SNAP). Use the National Council on Aging benefits check-up at www.BenefitsCheckUp.org.

Help her apply for those benefits. The Area Agency on Aging where Martina lives can help you find information. Find the local Area Agency on Aging through the Eldercare Locator at www.eldercare.gov.

Medicaid Is Complicated

Get legal advice and be very careful about decisions that may affect Martina's eligibility for Medicaid. The Medicaid program provides medical assistance and long-term care to low-income people. It may have another name in your state.

To find your state Medicaid agency, visit: www.benefits. gov/benefits/browse-by-category/category/MED.

Duty 3. Keep Martina's Money and Property Separate

Never mix Martina's money or property with your own or someone else's. Mixing money or property makes it unclear who owns what. Confused records can get you in trouble with Martina's family and also with government agencies such as adult protective services and the police or sheriff.

Follow these guidelines:

- Separate means separate. Never deposit Martina's money or property into your own or someone else's bank account or investment account.
- Avoid joint accounts. If Martina already has money or property in a joint account with you or someone else, get legal advice before making any change.
- Keep title to Martina's money and property in her own name. This is so other people can see right away that the money and property is Martina's and not yours.

- Know how to sign as agent~ Sign all checks and other documents relating to Martina's money or property to show that you are Martina's agent. For example, you might sign "Juan Doe, as agent for Martina Roe." Never just sign "Martina Roe."
- Pay Martina's expenses from her funds, not yours. Spending your money and then paying yourself back makes it hard to keep good records. If you really need to use your money, keep receipts for the expense and maintain a good record of why, what, and when you paid yourself.

Duty 4. Keep Good Records

You must keep true and complete records of Martina's money and property. The power of attorney or state law may say that someone else can review your records to check up on you.

Unless the power of attorney or state law says you can't share your records, you may want to let another family member or friend of Martina's see them as a precaution.

Practice good recordkeeping habits:

- *Keep a detailed list of everything that you receive or spend for Martina.* Records should include amount of checks written or deposited, dates, reasons, names of people or companies involved, and other important information.
- *Keep receipts and notes, even for small expenses.* For example, write "$50, groceries, ABC Grocery Store, May 2" in your records soon after you spend the money.
- *Avoid paying in cash.* Try not to pay Martina's expenses with cash. Also, try not to use her ATM card to withdraw cash or write checks to "Cash." If you need to use cash, be sure to keep receipts or notes.
- *Getting paid?* The power of attorney or state law may say that you can be paid for acting as agent. If you will be paid, be sure you charge a reasonable fee. It is up to you to keep detailed records as you go along of what work you did, how much time it took, when you did it, and why you did it.

More Things You Should Know

What If There Are Other Fiduciaries?

Co-Agents

Martina may have named one or more co-agents to act with you. The power of attorney document or state law should say whether you and any co-agents can make decisions alone or must agree on decisions, either unanimously or by majority rule.

Either way, you must coordinate with any co-agent and share information about decisions. Even if you and a co-agent don't have to agree on all decisions, you cannot let a co-agent do something that harms Martina. You are still responsible for her and must act in her best interest.

Successor Agents

Martina may have named a successor agent to act for her if you are not able to be the agent. A successor agent has no authority if you are still willing and able to act as Martina's agent.

Other Types of Fiduciary

Other fiduciaries may have authority to make decisions for Martina. For example, she may have a guardian of property, a representative payee who handles Social Security benefits, or a VA fiduciary who handles veterans benefits. It is important to work with these other fiduciaries, and keep them informed.

Government Benefits Require Special Fiduciaries

As agent, you cannot manage Martina's government benefits such as Social Security or VA benefits unless you get a separate appointment from the government agency as, for example, a representative payee or VA fiduciary. For more information, contact the government agency.

How Can You Avoid Problems with Family or Friends?

Family or friends may not agree with your decisions about Martina's money and property. To help reduce any friction, follow the four duties described above and the guidelines we've given you.

Sharing information may help. For example, you might want to share any accountings you prepare or summaries of how you've spent Martina's money, unless Martina has said that you should not. It usually is easier to deal with questions about a decision when it happens than to deal with suspicion and anger that may build over a long time. In the end, you have to make the final decisions.

Some family or friends may be so difficult that it is better not to share information with them. Use your best judgment.

If family or friends don't agree with your decisions, try to get someone to help sort it out—for example, a family counselor or mediator. See Where to go for help on page 22 of this guide.

What Should You Know About Working with Professionals?

In managing Martina's affairs, you may need help from professionals such as lawyers, brokers, financial advisors, accountants, real estate agents, appraisers, psychologists, social workers, doctors, nurses, or care managers. You can pay them with Martina's money. If you need help from any professionals, remember these tips:

- Check on the professional's qualifications. Many professionals must be licensed or registered by a government agency. Check credentials with the government agency. Make sure the license or registration is current and the professional is in good standing. Check the person's complaint history.
- Interview the professional thoroughly and ask questions.
- Review contracts carefully before signing. Before hiring any professionals, get their proposed plan of work and expected fee.
- Make your own decisions based on facts and advice. Listen to their advice, but remember you are the decision-maker.

Watch out for Financial Exploitation

Family, friends, neighbors, caregivers, fiduciaries, business people, and others may try to take advantage of Martina. They may take her money without permission, fail to repay money they owe, charge her too much for services, or just not do things she has paid them to do. These may be examples of financial exploitation or financial abuse. As Martina's agent, you should help protect her. You should know the signs of financial exploitation for five important reasons:

- Martina may still control some of her funds and could be exploited;
- Even if Martina does not control any of her funds, she still may be exploited;
- Martina may have been exploited already, and you may still be able to do something about that;
- People may try to take advantage of you as Martina's agent; and
- Knowing what to look for will help you avoid doing things you should not do, protecting you from claims that you have exploited Martina.

Look for These Common Signs of Financial Exploitation

- You think some money or property is missing.
- Martina says that some money or property is missing.
- You notice sudden changes in Martina's spending or savings. For example, she:
  - Takes out lots of money from the bank without explanation;
  - Tries to wire large amounts of money;
  - Uses the ATM a lot;
  - Is not able to pay bills that are usually paid;
  - Buys things or services that don't seem necessary;
  - Puts names on bank or other accounts that you do not recognize or that she is unwilling or unable to explain;
  - Does not get bank statements or bills;

  - Makes new or unusual gifts to family or others, such as a "new best friend";
  - Changes beneficiaries of a will, life insurance, or retirement funds; or
  - Has a caregiver, friend, or relative who suddenly begins handling her money. •

Martina says she is afraid or seems afraid of a relative, caregiver, or friend~

- A relative, caregiver, friend, or someone else keeps Martina from having visitors or phone calls, does not let her speak for herself, or seems to be controlling her decisions.

What Can You Do If Martina Has Been Exploited?

- Call the emergency 911 number if Martina is in immediate danger.
- Call local adult protective services or the police or sheriff. You may be required by law to do this.
- Alert Martina's bank or credit card company.
- Call the local prosecutor or state attorney general.
- Call the long-term care ombudsman program or the state Medicaid fraud control unit if Martina is in a nursing home or assisted living.
- Consider talking to a lawyer about protecting Martina from more exploitation or getting back money or property taken from her.
- Each agency or professional has a different role, so you may need to call more than one. For more information, see Where to go for help on page 22 of this guide.

Be on Guard for Consumer Scams

As Martina's agent, you should be alert to protect her money from consumer scams as well as financial exploitation. Criminals and con artists have many scams, and change them all the time. They often seek unsuspecting people who have access to money. Learn to spot consumer scams against Martina—and against you as her agent.

How Can You Protect Martina from Scams?

Consumer scams happen on the phone, through the mail, e-mail, or over the internet. They can occur in person, at home, or at a business. Here are some tips:

- Help Martina put her number on the National Do Not Call Registry. Go to www.donotcall.gov or call 1-888-382-1222.
- Don't share numbers or passwords for Martina's accounts, credit cards, or Social Security, unless you know whom you're dealing with and why they need the information.
- After hearing a sales pitch, take time to compare prices. Ask for information in writing and read it carefully.
- Too good to be true? Ask yourself why someone is trying so hard to give you a "great deal." If it sounds too good to be true, it probably is.
- Watch out for deals that are only "good today" and that pressure you to act quickly. Be suspicious if you are not given enough time to read a contract or get legal advice before signing. Also watch out if you are told that you need to pay the seller quickly, for example by wiring the money or sending it by courier.
- Never pay up front for a promised prize. Suspect a scam if you are required to pay fees or taxes to receive a prize or other financial windfall.
- Watch for signs Martina already has been scammed. For example, does she receive a lot of mail or e-mail for sweepstakes? Has she paid people you don't know, especially in other states or countries? Has she taken a lot of money out of the bank while she was with someone she recently met? Does she have a hard time explaining how she spent that money? Is she suddenly unable to pay for food, medicine, or utilities?

What Can You Do If Martina Has Been Scammed?

If you suspect a scam, get help. Contact a local, state, or federal agency, depending on the type of scam. You may also need to talk to a lawyer.

Local agencies to call are adult protective services, the long-term care ombudsman program, the police or sheriff, and the local Better Business Bureau.

State agencies to call are the office of the attorney general or another agency that deals with consumer protection.

Call a federal agency if scammers are in other states or countries. Federal agencies are the Consumer Financial Protection Bureau, the FBI, the Federal Trade Commission, or the U.S. Postal Inspection Service.

Each of these agencies and professionals has a different role so you may need to call more than one.

Common Consumer Scams	
Relative in need	Someone who pretends to be a family member or friend calls or e-mails you to say they are in trouble and need you to wire money right away.
Charity appeals	You get a call or letter from someone asking for money for a fake charity—either the charity does not exist or the charity did not call or write to you.
Lottery or sweepstakes	You get a call or e-mail that you have a chance to win a lot of money through a foreign country's sweepstakes or lottery. The caller will offer tips about how to win if you pay a fee or buy something. Or the caller or e-mail says you already have won and you must give your bank account information or pay a fee to collect your winnings.
Home improvement	Scammers take money for repairs and then they never return to do the work or they do bad work. Sometimes they break something to create more work or they say that things need work when they don't.
Free lunch	Scammers invite you to a free lunch and seminar, and then pressure you to give them information about your money, and to invest the money with them. They offer you "tips" or "guaranteed returns."
Free trip	Scammers say you've won a free trip but they ask for a credit card number or advance cash to hold the reservation.
Government money	You get a call or letter that seems to be from a government agency. Scammers say that if you give a credit card number or send a money order, you can apply for government help with housing, home repairs, utilities, or taxes.
Drug plans	Scammers pretend they are with Medicare prescription drug plans, and try to sell Medicare discount drug cards that are

Common Consumer Scams	
	not valid. Companies with Medicare drug plans are not allowed to send unsolicited mail, emails, or phone calls.
Identity theft	Scammers steal personal information—such as a name, date of birth, Social Security number, account number, and mother's maiden name— and use the information to open credit cards or get a mortgage in someone else's name.
Fake "official" mail	Scammers send letters or e-mails that look like they are from a legitimate bank, business, or agency to try to get your personal information or bank account number.

In: Money Management for Financial Caregivers ISBN: 978-1-63117-042-3
Editor: Olivia Crowder

Chapter 2

MANAGING SOMEONE ELSE'S MONEY: HELP FOR COURT-APPOINTED GUARDIANS OF PROPERTY AND CONSERVATORS*

American Bar Association Commission on Law and Aging

WHY READ THIS GUIDE?

Like many people, you may never have been a guardian of someone else's property before. That's why we created Managing someone else's money: Help for court-appointed guardians of property and conservators. This guide will help you understand what you can and cannot do in your role as a *guardian*. In that role, you are a *fiduciary*. For this guide, a fiduciary is anyone named to manage money or property for someone else. You'll find brief tips to help you avoid problems and resources for finding more information.

This guide is for family and friends serving as a guardian of property, not for professionals or organizations. The guide does not give you legal advice. State laws vary, so you may have additional duties. Talk to a lawyer if you have questions about your duties.

---

* This guide was developed under contract for the Consumer Financial Protection Bureau and released October 2013.

If you want to learn about how to become a guardian of property, this guide is not designed for you. Talk to a lawyer or read other guides from your state bar association or others.

Let's Start with a Scenario About How You Might Have Become a Guardian of Property

Your family member or friend may not be able to make decisions on his own about his money and property. For this guide, let's call him Martin. After a hearing, the court has named you *guardian of property* for Martin. You now have the duty and power to make decisions on Martin's behalf about some or all of his money and property.

The court has given you a lot of responsibility as Martin's guardian of property.

You are now a *fiduciary* with *fiduciary duties*.

What Is a Fiduciary?

Since you have been named to manage money or property for someone else, you are *a fiduciary*. The law requires you to manage Martin's money and property for HIS benefit, not yours. It does not matter if you are managing a lot of money or a little. It does not matter if you are a family member or not.

The role of a fiduciary carries with it legal responsibilities. When you act as a fiduciary for Martin, you have four basic duties that you must keep in mind:

1. Act only in Martin's best interest.
2. Manage Martin's money and property carefully.
3. Keep Martin's money and property separate from yours.
4. Keep good records.

As a fiduciary, you must be trustworthy, honest, and act in good faith. If you do not meet these standards, you could be removed as a fiduciary, sued, or have to repay money. It is even possible that the police or sheriff could investigate you and you could go to jail. *That's why it's always important to remember: It's not your money!*

Guardian of Property Questions and Answers

What Is a Guardian of Property?

A *guardian of property* is someone the court names to manage money and property for someone else whom the court has found cannot manage it alone.

Sometimes a guardian of property is also appointed as *guardian of the person*.

A guardian of the person makes Martin's health care and other personal decisions. Sometimes a different person is appointed to be the guardian of the person, or Martin himself may still be able to make these personal decisions.

This guide only covers duties of the guardian of property. *Terms can differ.* In many states a guardian of property may be called a *conservator* or *guardian of estate*. Martin's money and property is called his *estate*. A person under guardianship may be called an *incapacitated person, protected person* or *ward*.

Different Types of Fiduciaries Exist

In your role as guardian of property, you may act as or deal with other types of fiduciaries. These may include:

Trustees under a revocable living trust—someone names them to manage money and property.

Representative payees or, for veterans, VA fiduciaries—a government agency names them to manage government money that is paid to someone.

Agents under a power of attorney—someone names an agent to manage their money and property in case they are not able to do it.

What Are Your Responsibilities as a Guardian of Property?

As guardian of property, you have a double duty—both to Martin, the person you are serving, and to the court.

Duty to Martin

You must always keep Martin's best interests in mind. In managing his money, you must act for his good and not for your own good. Involve Martin in decisions as much as possible.

Duty to the Court

You are an agent of the court. The court has trusted you. You must report to the court regularly and be ready to answer any questions.

When Do Your Responsibilities End?

Your responsibilities as Martin's guardian of property last until the court relieves you of your duties. The court may do this because someone else has been appointed, Martin has died, or Martin no longer needs a guardian.

Don't Expect Others to Know What a Guardian of Property Is or Does

They may not understand that you have been appointed by the court. They may think you have more authority or less authority than you really have. You may need to educate them. You could show them this guide and a copy of the court order appointing you.

FOUR BASIC DUTIES OF A FIDUCIARY

Duty 1. Act Only in Martin's Best Interest

Because you are dealing with Martin's money and property, your duty is to make decisions that are best for him. This means you must ignore your own interests and needs, or the interests and needs of other people.

To help act in Martin's best interest, follow these guidelines:

- *Read the court order.* Your powers and duties as Martin's guardian of property are written in state law. They also may be written in the court order that appointed you. Some court orders may be detailed, while others may be very general. Read the court order closely, and talk to a lawyer if you don't understand it. In some states, a guardian is required to have a lawyer. Ask questions and learn all you can about what you should do—and what you should not do.

- *Do what the court order says—and don't do what it says you should not do.* It is important that you not act beyond what the law and the court order allow, and that you carry out the basic tasks necessary. Your powers may be limited to certain actions or certain amounts of money. You may need to get the court to approve other actions. Even if you have the best intentions, follow the court order.
- *As much as possible, involve Martin in decisions.* Many things can affect your decisions. For example, you might feel pressure from others. Martin's abilities to make decisions might change from time to time, or maybe Martin was never able to make decisions about his money and property. Consider these three steps:
  - First, ask Martin what he wants. He may be able to decide some things. If so, take this into account, especially if it is similar to his thinking in the past and the risk of harm to him is not unreasonable. For example, if Martin wants to handle money, see if he can manage a small bank account or a monthly cash allowance. Doing this will let him be in charge of a set amount, and you will limit the risk to that amount.
  - Second, try to find out what Martin would have wanted. Look at any past decisions, actions, and statements. Find as much information as you can. Ask people who care about Martin what they think he would have wanted. Make the decision you think that Martin would have made, unless doing so would harm him.
  - Third, do what you think is best for him. If you have looked hard and still don't know what Martin would have wanted— or if Martin could never make decisions about money and property—use your judgment about what is best. Put Martin's well-being above saving money for others who may inherit his money and property. Make sure that he is safe and comfortable, and his needs are met.
- *Avoid conflicts of interest.* A conflict of interest happens if you make a decision about Martin's property that may benefit someone else at Martin's expense. Because you were appointed by the court, you have a strict duty to avoid conflicts of interest—or even the appearance of a

conflict of interest. Try to keep an "arm's length distance" between your interests and any use of Martin's money.

- *Don't borrow, loan, or give Martin's money to yourself or others~* Even if the court order clearly allows gifts to you or others, be very careful to avoid conflicts of interest. Usually, the court must approve gifts or loans, or those over a certain amount. Make sure that any gifts do not increase or complicate Martin's taxes or change his plans for his property when he dies. Any gifts or loans should be in line with what Martin would have wanted. For example, if Martin gave money every year to a charity, the court may allow you to continue doing that.
- *Avoid changing Martin's plans for giving away his money or property when he dies.* There may be rare situations when changing Martin's plans is in his best interest. But you should get legal advice and approval from the court before you do anything.
- *Don't pay yourself for the time you spend acting as Martin's guardian of property, unless the court allows you to do so.* If you are allowed to pay yourself, get legal advice, check with the court, and carefully document how much time you spend and what you do.

Avoid Possible Conflicts of Interest

Sometimes people have good intentions, but do things they shouldn't. Because you are now a fiduciary, you should avoid any conflicts of interest. Here are a few examples of possible conflicts of interest:

Whose Car Is It?

You used Martin's money to buy a car. You use it to drive him to appointments, but most of the time you drive the car just for your own needs. This may be a conflict of interest.

Should You Do Business with Family?

Martin needs repair work in his apartment. You hire your son and pay him from Martin's money. This may be a conflict of interest, even though the work was needed. It appears that you have put your personal interest to benefit your son in conflict with Martin's interests.

To avoid any surprises or misunderstandings, tell family about your fees when you begin your duties as a guardian of property. Don't charge fees that are overly high, and don't charge for things you do that are not specifically as guardian of property. For instance, don't charge fees if you shop for Martin or personally make home repairs. If necessary, you can pay someone else at a lower rate for these tasks and document the expenses.

DUTY 2. MANAGE MARTIN'S MONEY AND PROPERTY CAREFULLY

Tips For Making an Inventory

- *Don't leave anything out.* Even if you know Martin wants you to have certain things and says so in his will, list them in the inventory. A proper inventory lists everything according to the court's rules. Do not decide that some things should not be listed.
- *Search carefully.* Look carefully to find everything Martin owns. Search his mail and home. Look for real estate by talking to family or advisors and looking through land records. Track down letters from creditors to find unpaid debts.
- *Take valuable items to an appraiser.*
- *Verify if necessary.* It is a good idea to have someone else check the list, especially if family might argue over Martin's money and property.

As Martin's guardian of property, you might pay bills, oversee bank accounts, or pay for things he needs. You might also make investments, pay taxes, collect rent or unpaid debts, get insurance if needed, cancel any unneeded insurance, and do other things in the court order.

You have a duty to manage Martin's money and property very carefully. Use good judgment and common sense. As a fiduciary, you must be even more careful with Martin's money than you might be with your own!

Follow these guidelines strictly according to the court's procedures:

- Make an inventory. To make careful decisions, you need to know what Martin owns and owes. To make a proper inventory, you must find and list for the court all of Martin's income and property, as well as any debts or legal claims against his properties (called liens.) The court may give you a form and a deadline for making the inventory—

for example, you might have 3 months. To avoid any risk to Martin's money and property, you must make the inventory as quickly as possible.

An inventory may include all kinds of property. Your list might include:

- Checking and savings accounts;
- Cash;
- Pension, retirement, annuity, rental, public benefit, or other income;
- Real estate;
- Cars and other vehicles;
- Insurance policies;
- Trusts for which Martin is a beneficiary;
- Stocks and bonds;
- Jewelry, furniture, and any other items of value; and
- Unpaid credit card bills and other outstanding loans.

- File the inventory with the court. Keep a copy of the inventory for your records and file it with the court by the due date. Be ready to share it with family listed with the court as interested parties. In some states, you must have a lawyer review and sign the inventory.
- The court will probably require you to buy a bond. The court may require you to buy a bond. A bond is a special type of insurance policy so the court can make sure you carry out your duties. If you fail in your duties and, as a result, money is lost or stolen, the bonding company will pay the money back. Then the company will try to collect the money from you. The cost of the bond may be payable from Martin's money. Ask the court staff whether you may use Martin's money to cover this expense.

Only people with good financial records and credit histories can get a bond. If you have had a bankruptcy, you will not likely be able to get a bond. Try to check this before you are appointed as guardian of property or as soon as possible. Take all steps the court advises about getting a bond.

Sometimes, instead of requiring a bond, the court will limit the amount of funds you can take out of Martin's account. This is called a restricted account. The court will tell the bank to block the account above a certain amount. If you want to spend more than that amount, you must get the court to approve the expense.

- Protect Martin's property. Keep his money and property safe. Have Martin's income and bills sent to you. Put his valuable items in safe deposit boxes and lock other items he is not using in storage. Keep Martin's cash in bank accounts that earn interest if possible and that have low or no fees. Review bank and other financial statements promptly. If Martin will not be living in his home, consider changing the locks. Figure out if the house should be rented, or how to keep it safe if it is vacant. If Martin rented an apartment and will be moving, tell the landlord, remove his things, and have the apartment cleaned.
- Make a financial plan. Make a budget as if you were making one for your own household. List how much you expect to pay for nursing home, assisted living or home care, rent, food, medical care, and home maintenance or repair. Be sure to include a monthly amount for Martin to use as he pleases. Think about any special expenses that may arise, such as dental work or any medical care or equipment that Medicare, Medicaid, or other health insurance will not cover. Try to stick to your budget. If something very costly occurs, you may need the court to approve the expense.
- *Invest carefully*. If you are making investments for Martin, talk to a financial professional. The Securities and Exchange Commission (SEC) provides tips on choosing a financial professional at www.sec.gov/investor/alerts/ib_top_tips.pdf. Discuss your choices and goals for investing based on Martin's needs and values.
- *Pay bills and taxes on time.*
- *Cancel any insurance policies that Martin does not need.*
- *Collect debts*. Find out if anyone owes Martin money, and try to collect it.
- There's no place like home. Your state's law or the court order may not allow you to sell Martin's real estate. In any case, it is good practice to get court approval to sell, mortgage, or lease any property.
- *Martin may want to continue to live in the home he owns or rents*. In that case, take these steps:
  - Determine if living in his home is safe, and if Martin can manage in the house. If needed, put in guard rails, grab bars, smoke detectors, extra lighting, and other things to help him stay at home.

Tax credits or deductions might be available if you make the home easier to live in. Work with any other decision-makers (such as an agent under a health care power of attorney or any guardian of the person if you have not been appointed to fill this role).

If it is not safe to live at home even with changes—or if Martin wants to move— *consider other places that meet Martin's needs.* Try to keep him connected to people and things important to him. Choices might be living with someone else, or living in a retirement community, a senior apartment, group home, assisted living, or nursing home. You may need court approval for a move.

Can Martin Get Any Benefits?

Find out if Martin is eligible for any financial or health care benefits from an employer or a government. These benefits might include pensions, disability, Social Security, Medicare, Medicaid, Veterans benefits, housing assistance, or food stamps (now known as Supplemental Nutrition Assistance Program or SNAP). Use the National Council on Aging benefits check-up at www.BenefitsCheckUp.org.

Help him apply for those benefits. The Area Agency on Aging where Martin lives can help you find information. Find the local Area Agency on Aging through the Eldercare Locator at www.eldercare.gov.

Medicaid Is Complicated

Get legal advice and be very careful about decisions that may affect Martin's eligibility for Medicaid. The Medicaid program provides medical assistance and long-term care to low-income people. It may have another name in your state. To find your state Medicaid agency, visit: www.benefits.gov/benefits/browse-by-category/category/MED.

Duty 3. Keep Martin's Money and Property Separate

Never mix Martin's money or property with your own or someone else's. Mixing money or property makes it unclear who owns what. Confused records can get you in trouble with the court.

Follow these guidelines:

- Separate means separate. Never deposit Martin's money into your own or someone else's bank account or investment account.
- Avoid joint accounts. If Martin already has money in a joint account with you or someone else, get legal advice before making any change.
- Keep title to Martin's money and property in his own name. This is so other people can see right away that the money and property is Martin's and not yours. Ask the bank for a guardianship or fiduciary account that shows you are managing the account for Martin.
  - Know how to sign as guardian. Sign all checks and other documents relating to Martin's money or property to show that you are Martin's guardian. For example, you might sign: "Juan Doe, as guardian for Martin Roe." Never just sign "Martin Roe."
  - Pay Martin's expenses from his funds, not yours. Spending your money and then paying yourself back makes it hard to keep good records. If you really need to use your money, save receipts for the expense and keep a good record of why, what, and when you paid yourself.

Duty 4. Keep Good Records and Report to the Court

You must keep true and complete records of Martin's money and property.

As guardian of property, the court or a lawsuit can challenge you to show everything you've done with Martin's money and property. Always be ready to share your records with family—unless you think they will misuse the information to harm Martin.

Practice good recordkeeping habits:

- *Keep a detailed list of everything that you receive or spend for Martin.* Records should include the amount of checks written or deposited, dates, reasons, names of people or companies involved, and other important information.
- *Keep receipts and notes, even for small expenses.* For example, write "$50, groceries, ABC Grocery Store, May 2" in your records soon after you spend the money.

- *Avoid paying in cash.* Try not to pay Martin's expenses with cash. Also, try not to use an ATM card to withdraw cash or write checks to "Cash." If you need to use cash, be sure to keep receipts or notes.
- *Getting paid? If you are permitted by the court to charge a fee to serve as guardian of property, be sure you charge a reasonable fee.* Keep detailed records as you go along of what work you did, how much time it took, when you did it, and why you did it.
- *File your accountings with the court.* Each year—or whenever the court requires— you must report to the court, including giving an accounting of all the money you received and spent.
  - The court will give you a specific form for the accounting or will tell you what is required. Use the records you have kept during the year to fill in the form. If you have questions, ask court staff or a lawyer for help.
  - The court will tell you when the accounting is due. Be sure to turn it in on time. If your accounting is late, the court may call you in to explain why.
  - Your accounting must be clear and must "add up." The accounting should show a beginning balance, income during the year, expenses during the year, and an ending balance. The ending balance for one year should be the same as the beginning balance for the next year.
  - Accounting requirements differ by court, and may change over time. Try to understand in advance what is needed, so that your accounting is not rejected for a minor problem. Ask for an example of a correct accounting. You may need an accountant to help.
- File a final accounting after Martin dies. Notify the court when Martin dies. According to court procedures, make a final accounting of Martin's money and property, and ask for an order releasing you from your duties.
  - Sometimes, you may need to pay final bills or make final arrangements, especially if no one else can do it. For example, you may need to pay funeral expenses and final medical bills.
  - ú If Martin did not already make funeral or burial arrangements, look for any directions he may have left—perhaps in advance directives or remarks to family or friends.

– An executor named in a will, an administrator named by the court, or a trustee named in a trust will handle Martin's money and property after you turn them over. Hold Martin's personal things safely until they are transferred to whoever is to receive them. If you are the one named to handle Martin's money and property after his death, make sure you understand when your duties as guardian end and your new duties begin.

More Things You Should Know

What if There Are Other Fiduciaries?

Co-Guardians

The court may have named someone else to act with you as Martin's guardian of property, or it may have named someone else to act as Martin's guardian of person to make healthcare and other personal decisions.

Any other guardians will be your partners in making decisions on Martin's behalf and in helping him make decisions if he is able. You must work closely together. For example, if Martin will move to a new location or get special care, his guardians must make important personal and financial decisions. You must consult with one another.

Other Types of Fiduciaries

Other fiduciaries may have authority to make decisions for Martin. For example, he may have an agent under a power of attorney, a representative payee who handles Social Security benefits, or a VA fiduciary who handles veterans benefits. It is important to work with these other fiduciaries, and keep them informed.

Government Benefits Require Special Fiduciaries

As guardian of property, you cannot manage Martin's government benefits such as Social Security or VA benefits unless you get a separate appointment from the government agency as, for example, a representative payee or VA fiduciary. For more information, contact the government agency.

How Can You Avoid Problems with Family or Friends?

Family or friends may not agree with your decisions about Martin's money and property. To help reduce any friction, follow the four duties described above and the guidelines we've given you.

- Sharing information may help (unless Martin has said that you should not). It usually is easier to deal with questions about a decision when it happens than to deal with suspicion and anger that may build over a long time. State law or the court may require you to send accountings to family and friends, or may say you should not. If there is no direction from the court, get court approval before sharing information.
- Some family or friends may not have Martin's best interest at heart, so it may be better not to share information with them, or to ask the court not to share it. Use your best judgment.
- If family or friends don't agree with your decisions, try to get someone to help sort it out—for example, a family counselor or mediator. See Where to go for help on page 26 of this guide.

What Should You Know About Working with Professionals?

In managing Martin's affairs, you may need help from professionals such as lawyers, brokers, financial advisors, accountants, real estate agents, appraisers, psychologists, social workers, doctors, nurses, or care managers. You can pay them with Martin's money.

If you need help from any professionals, remember these tips:

- *Check on the professional's qualifications.* Many professionals must be licensed or registered by a government agency. Check credentials with the government agency. Make sure the license or registration is current and the professional is in good standing. Check the person's complaint history.
- *Interview the professional thoroughly and ask questions.*
- *Review contracts carefully before signing.* Before hiring any professionals, get their proposed plan of work and expected fee.

- *Make your own decisions based on facts and advice*. Listen to their advice but remember you are the decision-maker.

WATCH OUT FOR FINANCIAL EXPLOITATION

Family, friends, neighbors, caregivers, fiduciaries, business people, and others may try to take advantage of Martin. They may take his money without permission, neglect to repay money they owe, charge him too much for services, or just not do things he has paid them to do. These may be examples of financial exploitation or financial abuse. As Martin's guardian of property, you should help protect him. You should know the signs of financial exploitation for five important reasons:

1. Martin may still control some of his funds and could be exploited;
2. Even if Martin does not control any of his funds, he still may be exploited;
3. Martin may have been exploited already, and you may still be able to do something about that;
4. People may try to take advantage of you as Martin's guardian; and
5. Knowing what to look for will help you avoid doing things you should not do, protecting you from claims that you have exploited Martin.

Look for These Common Signs of Financial Exploitation

- Some money or property is missing.
- Martin says that some money or property is missing.
- You notice sudden changes in Martin's spending or savings. For example, he:
  - Takes out lots of money from the bank without explanation;
  - Tries to wire large amounts of money;
  - Uses the ATM a lot;
  - Is not able to pay bills that are usually paid;
  - Buys things or services that don't seem necessary;
  - Puts names on bank or other accounts that you do not recognize or that he is unwilling or unable to explain;

  - Does not get bank statements or bills;
  - Makes new or unusual gifts to family or others, such as a "new best friend";
  - Changes beneficiaries of a will, life insurance, or retirement funds; or
  - Has a caregiver, friend, or relative who suddenly begins handling his money.
- Martin says he is afraid or seems afraid of a relative, caregiver, or friend.
- A relative, caregiver, friend, or someone else keeps Martin from having visitors or phone calls, or does not let him speak for himself, or seems to be controlling his decisions.

What Can You Do if Martin Has Been Exploited?

- Call the emergency 911 number if Martin is in immediate danger.
- Call local adult protective services or the police or sheriff. You may be required by law to do this.
- Alert Martin's bank or credit card company.
- Call the local prosecutor or state attorney general.
- Call the long-term care ombudsman program or the state Medicaid fraud control unit if Martin is in a nursing home or assisted living.
- Consider talking to a lawyer about protecting Martin from more exploitation or getting back money or property taken from him.

Each agency or professional has a different role, so you may need to call more than one. For more information, see Where to go for help on page 26 of this guide.

Be on Guard for Consumer Scams

As Martin's guardian of property, you should be alert to protect his money from consumer scams as well as financial exploitation. Criminals and con artists have many scams, and change them all the time. They often seek unsuspecting people who have access to money. Learn to spot consumer scams against Martin—and against you as his guardian.

How Can You Protect Martin from Scams?

Consumer scams happen on the phone; through the mail, e-mail, or the Internet; and they occur in person, at home, or at a business.

Here are some tips:

- *Put Martin's number on the National Do Not Call Registry.* Go to www. donotcall.gov or call 1-888-382-1222.
- *Don't share numbers or passwords for Martin's accounts, credit cards, or Social Security,* unless you know whom you're dealing with and why they need the information.
- *After hearing a sales pitch, take time to compare prices.* Ask for information in writing and read it carefully.
- *Too good to be true? Ask yourself why someone is trying so hard to give you a "great deal."* If it sounds too good to be true, it probably is.
- *Watch out for deals that are only "good today" and that pressure you to act quickly.* Be suspicious if you are not given enough time to read a contract or get legal advice before signing. Also watch out if you are told that you need to pay the seller quickly, for example by wiring the money or sending it by courier.
- *Never pay up front for a promised prize.* Suspect a scam if you are required to pay fees or taxes to receive a prize or other financial windfall.
- *Watch for signs Martin already has been scammed.* For example, does he receive a lot of mail or e-mail for sweepstakes? Has he paid people you don't know, especially in other states or countries? Has he taken a lot of money out of the bank while he was with someone he recently met? Does he have a hard time explaining how he spent that money? Is he suddenly unable to pay for food, medicine, or utilities?

What Can You Do if Martin Has Been Scammed?

If you suspect a scam, get help. Contact a local, state, or federal agency, depending on the type of scam. You may also need to talk to a lawyer.

Local agencies to call are adult protective services, the long-term care ombudsman program, the police or sheriff, and the local Better Business Bureau.

State agencies to call are the office of the attorney general or another agency that deals with consumer protection.

Call a federal agency if scammers are in other states or countries. Federal agencies are the Consumer Financial Protection Bureau, the FBI, the Federal Trade Commission, or the U.S. Postal Inspection Service.

Each of these agencies and professionals has a different role so you may need to call more than one.

In: Money Management for Financial Caregivers ISBN: 978-1-63117-042-3
Editor: Olivia Crowder

Chapter 3

MANAGING SOMEONE ELSE'S MONEY: HELP FOR TRUSTEES UNDER A REVOCABLE LIVING TRUST*

American Bar Association Commission on Law and Aging

WHY READ THIS GUIDE?

Like many people, you may never have been a trustee under a revocable living trust before. That's why we created Managing someone else's money: Help for trustees under a revocable living trust. This guide will help you understand what you can and cannot do in your role as a trustee. In that role, you are a fiduciary. For this guide, a fiduciary is anyone named to manage money or property for someone else. You'll find brief tips to help you avoid problems and resources for finding more information.

This guide is for family and friends serving as a trustee, not for professionals or organizations. The guide does not give you legal advice. State laws vary, so you may have additional or different duties. Talk to a lawyer if you have questions about your duties.

---

* This guide was developed under contract for the Consumer Financial Protection Bureau and released October 2013.

If you want to learn about making a revocable living trust, this guide is not designed for you. Talk to a lawyer or read other guides about revocable living trusts from your state bar association or others.

Let's Start with a Scenario About How You Might Have Become a Trustee

Your family member or friend is worried that she will get sick and will not be able to pay her bills or make other decisions about her savings and her house. For this guide, we will call her Rose. Rose has signed a legal document called a *living trust.* In it, she names you as her *trustee.*

When she set up the trust, she should have transferred ownership of some or all her money and property from her name to the name of the trust. As her trustee, you now have the power to make decisions for Rose's benefit about the money and property in the trust.

The law gives you a lot of responsibility. You are now a *fiduciary* with *fiduciary duties.*

What Is a Fiduciary?

Since you have been named to manage money or property for someone else, you are a fiduciary. The law requires you to manage the money and property in the trust for Rose's benefit, not yours. It does not matter if you are managing a lot of money or a little. It does not matter if you are family or not.

The role of a fiduciary carries with it legal responsibilities. When you act as a fiduciary for Rose, you have four basic duties that you must keep in mind:

1. Act only in Rose's best interest.
2. Manage the money and property in the trust carefully.
3. Keep the trust property separate from yours.
4. Keep good records.

As a fiduciary, you must be trustworthy, honest, and act in good faith. If you do not meet these standards, you could be removed as a fiduciary, sued, or you might have to repay money. It is even possible that the police or sheriff could investigate you and you could go to jail. That's why it's always important to remember: It's not your money!

Different Types of Fiduciaries Exist

In your role as trustee, you may act as or deal with other types of fiduciaries. These may include:

Agents under a power of attorney—someone names an agent to manage their money and property in case they are not able to do it.

Representative payees or, for veterans, VA fiduciaries—a government agency names them to manage government money that is paid to someone.

Guardians or conservators—a court names them to manage money and property for someone who needs help.

Revocable Living Trust Questions and Answers

What Is a Revocable Living Trust?

A revocable living trust is a legal document. Rose made a revocable living trust to give you legal authority to make decisions about her money or property in the trust if she cannot make decisions herself because she is sick or injured. She also made the revocable living trust to say who will get her money or property after she dies. In some states, the term "living trust" is used to mean a different type of trust than a "revocable living trust." But in the rest of this guide we use "living trust" or "trust" as shorthand for "revocable living trust."

There are three roles under a revocable living trust.

- The person who makes the trust may be called the settlor, grantor or trustor.
- The person who makes decisions about the money or property in the revocable living trust is called the trustee. A trustee can be an individual or a financial institution. If there is more than one, they are co-trustees. A successor trustee may also be named and acts only if a trustee can no longer fulfill that role. Rose can name herself as trustee and you as co-trustee immediately, or you may be a successor trustee who can act when she can no longer make decisions.
- A person who receives money or property from the revocable living trust is called a beneficiary. Rose may be the only beneficiary while she is alive, or she may name co-beneficiaries who receive some

money or property from the revocable living trust before she dies. The people who receive money or benefits from the revocable living trust after Rose dies are called residuary beneficiaries.

What Property Does a Trustee Manage?

The trustee has authority only over property actually transferred to the revocable living trust and only after Rose has lost the capacity to manage her property. A living trust is ineffective unless Rose puts her money or property into it. Some state laws require Rose to change ownership of her money or property from her name to the name of the revocable living trust (for example, the "Rose Roe Living Trust"). In other states, Rose must switch ownership from her name to the name of the trustee who holds the property for the revocable living trust. When you are acting as trustee you will have the legal authority to spend and invest the money and property in the revocable living trust for the benefit of Rose and any other beneficiaries. You do not have legal authority over any money or property that is not in the trust.

Don't Expect Others to Know What a Trustee Is or Does

They may not understand that you have been named as a trustee. They may think that you have more authority or less authority than you really have. You may need to educate them. You could show them this guide.

Can a Revocable Living Trust Be Changed or Revoked?

As long as Rose still can make her own decisions and the terms of the trust allow her to do so, she can change or end (revoke) the revocable living trust.

When Do Your Responsibilities End?

If Rose names a new trustee or ends the trust, your authority and responsibilities end.

What If You Think a Change in the Trust Was a Result of Fraud or Abuse?

If you think Rose does not understand the decision to take away your authority or end the trust, then talk to a lawyer, contact adult protective services, or call the police or sheriff.

Aren't There Other Types of Trusts?

Yes. Other types of trusts exist and people have different reasons for making trusts. This guide only covers living trusts.

Living trusts most likely have family or a friend as a trustee. Other types of trust often have professional trustees, such as a lawyer or bank trust officer.

Four Basic Duties of a Fiduciary

Avoid Possible Conflicts of Interest

Sometimes people have good intentions, but do things they shouldn't. Because you are now a fiduciary, you should avoid any conflicts of interest. Here are a few examples of possible conflicts of interest:

Should You Sell Trust Assets to Yourself?

Selling trust assets to yourself is usually seen as a conflict of interest (called self-dealing). Talk to a lawyer before doing this.

Should You Do Business with Family?

Like most people, Rose needs homeowners' insurance. Because your spouse sells insurance, you decide to buy Rose's insurance from him without shopping around for better coverage or prices from other insurance agents. This may be a conflict of interest.

Duty 1. Act Only in Rose's Best Interest

Because you are dealing with the trust's money and property, your duty is to make decisions that are best for Rose and any co-beneficiaries. This means you must ignore your own interests and needs, or the interests and needs of other people.

To help act in Rose's best interest, follow these guidelines:

- Read the living trust document and do what it says. Your authority is limited to what the document and state law allow. There may be duties required by state law even if they are not in the living trust document. Talk to a lawyer if there is anything you don't understand. Follow Rose's directions in the trust document even if you have the best intentions in wanting to do something different.
- Understand when your duty as trustee becomes effective. The living trust may say that you become a trustee or a co-trustee right away or only when Rose can no longer make her own decisions. Check to see if the document says how you will know when Rose can no longer make her own decisions. If you are still unsure, get legal advice.
- Avoid conflicts of interest. A conflict of interest happens if you make a decision about Rose's money or property in the trust that may benefit someone else at Rose's expense. As a fiduciary, you have a strict duty to avoid conflicts of interest— or even the appearance of a conflict of interest.
- Don't borrow, loan, or give the trust's money to yourself or others. Even if state law or the trust document allows gifts or loans, consider whether the trust can afford the gifts or loans, and whether they are in line with what Rose would have wanted. A lawyer can advise you on any effects on Rose's taxes or on her plans to give away her property when she dies.
- Avoid changing Rose's plans for giving away her money or property when she dies. There may be rare situations in which changing Rose's plans would be in her best interest. But you should get legal advice to make sure that the trust document or state law allows that.
- Don't pay yourself for the time you spend acting as Rose's trustee, unless the living trust or state law allows it. If you are allowed to pay yourself, you need to show that your fee is reasonable. Carefully document how much time you spend and what you do.

Duty 2. Manage the Money and Property in the Trust Carefully

- As Rose's trustee, you might pay bills, oversee bank accounts, and pay for things she needs. You might also make investments, pay taxes, collect rent or unpaid debts, get insurance if needed, and do other things written in the living trust or required by state law.
- You have a duty to manage the money and property in the trust very carefully. Use good judgment and common sense. As a fiduciary, you must be even more careful with the trust's money than you might be with your own!
- Follow these guidelines to help you make careful decisions:
- *List the trust's money, property, and debts.* You need to know what Rose's trust owns and owes to make careful decisions. Your list might include:
  - Checking and savings accounts;
  - Cash;
  - Pension, retirement, annuity, rental, public benefit, or other income;
  - Real estate;
  - Cars and other vehicles;
  - Insurance policies;
  - Stocks and bonds;
  - Jewelry, furniture, and any other items of value;
  - Unpaid credit card bills and other outstanding loans.

The living trust or state law may require you to share the list with a beneficiary or with someone else.

- *Protect the trust's property.* Keep the trust's money and property safe. You may need to put valuable items in safe deposit boxes, change locks on property, and make sure her home or other property is insured. Make sure bank accounts earn interest if possible and have low or no fees. Review bank and other financial statements promptly. If the trust has real estate, keep it in good condition.
- *Invest carefully.* Talk to a financial professional or lawyer about safe and legal ways to invest the trust's assets. The Securities and Exchange Commission (SEC) provides tips on choosing a financial professional at www.sec.gov/investor/ alerts/ib_top_

tips.pdf. Discuss choices and goals for investing based on Rose's needs and values.

- *Pay bills and taxes on time.*
- *Cancel any insurance policies that Rose does not need.*
- *Collect debts.* Find out if anyone owes the trust money, and try to collect it.

Can Rose Get Any Benefits?

Find out if Rose is eligible for any financial or health care benefits from an employer or a government. These benefits might include pensions, disability, Social Security, Medicare, Medicaid, Veterans benefits, housing assistance, or food stamps (now known as Supplemental Nutrition Assistance Program or SNAP). Use the National Council on Aging benefits check-up at: www.BenefitsCheckUp.org.

Help her apply for those benefits. The Area Agency on Aging where Rose lives can help you find information. Find the local Area Agency on Aging through the Eldercare Locator at www.eldercare.gov.

Medicaid Is Complicated

Get legal advice and be very careful about decisions that may affect Rose's eligibility for Medicaid. The Medicaid program provides medical assistance and long-term care to low-income people. It may have another name in your state. To find your state Medicaid agency, visit: www.benefits.gov/benefits/browse-by-category/category/MED.

Duty 3. Keep the Trust Property Separate

Never mix money or property in Rose's trust with your own or someone else's. Mixing money or property makes it unclear who owns what. Confused records can get you in trouble with Rose's family and also with government agencies such as adult protective services and the police or sheriff.

Follow these guidelines:

- *Separate means separate.* Never deposit the trust's money into your own or someone else's bank account or investment account.

- *Never hold title to the trust's money and property in your own name.* Every document should show the owner of the assets as either the Rose Roe Living Trust or your name as trustee of the Rose Roe Living Trust. This is so other people can see right away that the money and property belongs to the trust and not to you.
- *Know how to sign as trustee.* Sign all checks and other documents relating to the trust's money or property to show that you are Rose's trustee. For example, you might sign "John Doe, as trustee for the Rose Roe Living Trust." Never just sign "Rose Roe."
- *Pay Rose's expenses from the trust funds, not yours.* Spending your money and then paying yourself back makes it hard to keep good records. If you really need to use your money, keep receipts for the expense and maintain a good record of why, what, and when you paid yourself back.

Duty 4. Keep Good Records

You must keep true and complete records of the money and property in Rose's living trust. The living trust document or state law may say that you must share your records with someone else who can check up on you.

Practice good recordkeeping habits:

- *Keep a detailed list of everything the trust receives and spends.* Records should include amount of checks written or deposited, dates, reasons, names of people or companies involved, and other important information.
- *Keep receipts and notes, even for small expenses.* For example, write "$50, groceries, ABC Grocery Store, May 2" in your records, soon after you spend the money.
- *Avoid paying in cash.* Try not to pay Rose's expenses with cash. Also, try not to use an ATM card to withdraw cash or write checks to "Cash." If you need to use cash, be sure to keep receipts and notes.
  - Getting paid? The living trust document or state law may say that you can be paid for acting as trustee. If you will be paid, be sure you are charging a reasonable fee. Keep detailed records, as you go along, of what work you did, how much time it took, when you did it, and why you did it.

MORE THINGS YOU SHOULD KNOW

What if There Are Other Fiduciaries?

Co-Trustees

Rose may have named herself as co-trustee with you. Or she may have named someone else to act as co-trustee with you. The living trust document or state law should say whether you and any co-trustees can make decisions alone or must agree on decisions, either unanimously or by majority rule.

Either way, you must coordinate with any co-trustee and share information about decisions. Even if you and a co-trustee don't agree on all decisions, you cannot let a co-trustee do something that harms Rose. You are still responsible for her and must act in her best interest.

Successor Agents

Rose may have named a successor trustee to act for her if you are not able to be the trustee. A successor trustee has no authority if you are still willing and able to act as trustee.

Other Types of Fiduciary

Other fiduciaries may have authority to make decisions for Rose. For example, she may have a guardian of property, a representative payee who handles Social Security benefits, or a VA fiduciary who handles veterans benefits. It is important to work with these other fiduciaries, and keep them informed.

Government Benefits Require Special Fiduciaries

As trustee, you cannot manage Rose's government benefits such as Social Security or Veterans benefits, unless:

1. Her benefits are paid directly into her trust, or
2. You have been appointed by the government agency as, for example, a representative payee or VA Fiduciary to handle these benefits. For more information, contact the government agency.

More Than One Beneficiary?

If Rose named more than one beneficiary of her living trust, then you have fiduciary duties to each beneficiary. The living trust document and state law will say what your duties are to the beneficiaries.

You must always be impartial when you carry out your duties as Rose's trustee. You cannot show any bias toward any one beneficiary. Because each beneficiary's needs are different, you do not have to treat everyone the same. But you must act in each beneficiary's best interest in an unbiased way.

Talk to a lawyer about what your duties are if Rose's trust has named more than one beneficiary.

How Can You Avoid Problems with Family or Friends?

Family or friends may not agree with your decisions about money and property in Rose's trust. To help reduce any friction, follow the four duties described above and the guidelines we've given you.

Sharing information may help. For example, you might want to share any accountings you prepare or summaries of how you've spent the trust's money, unless Rose has said you should not. It usually is easier to deal with questions about a decision when it happens than to deal with suspicion and anger that may build over a long time. In the end, you have to make the final decisions.

Some family or friends may be so difficult that it is better not to share information with them. Use your best judgment.

If family or friends don't agree with your decisions, try to get someone to help sort it out—for example, a family counselor or mediator. See *Where to go for help* on page 24 of this guide.

What Should You Know About Working with Professionals?

In managing the trust's affairs, you may need help from professionals such as lawyers, brokers, financial advisors, accountants, real estate agents, appraisers, psychologists, social workers, doctors, nurses, or care managers. You can pay them with money from the trust.

If you need help from any professionals, remember these tips:

- Check on the professional's qualifications. Many professionals must be licensed or registered by a government agency. Check credentials with the government agency. Make sure the license or registration is current and the professional is in good standing. Check the person's complaint history.
- Interview the professional thoroughly and ask questions.
- Review contracts carefully before signing. Before hiring any professionals, get their proposed plan of work and expected fee.
- Make your own decisions based on facts and advice. Listen to their advice, but remember you are the decision-maker.

Watch Out for Financial Exploitation

Family, friends, neighbors, caregivers, fiduciaries, business people, and others may try to take advantage of Rose. They may take her money without permission, neglect to repay money they owe, charge her too much for services, or just not do things she has paid them to do. If any of these happen, it may be examples of *financial exploitation* or *financial abuse*. As Rose's trustee, you should help protect her and know the signs of financial exploitation for five important reasons:

1. Rose may still control some of her funds and could be exploited;
2. Even if Rose does not control any of her funds, she still may be exploited;
3. Rose may have been exploited already, and you may still be able to do something about that;
4. People may try to take advantage of you as Rose's trustee; and
5. Knowing what to look for will help you avoid doing things you should not do, protecting you from claims that you have exploited Rose.

Look for These Common Signs of Financial Exploitation

- You think some money or property is missing.
- Rose says that some money or property is missing.

- You notice sudden changes in Rose's spending or savings. For example, she:
  - Takes out lots of money from the bank without explanation;
  - Tries to wire large amounts of money;
  - Uses the ATM a lot;
  - Is not able to pay bills that are usually paid;
  - Buys things or services that don't seem necessary;

  - Takes out lots of money from the bank without explanation;
  - Tries to wire large amounts of money;
  - Uses the ATM a lot;
  - Is not able to pay bills that are usually paid;
  - Buys things or services that don't seem necessary;

  - Puts names on bank or other accounts that you do not recognize or that she is unwilling or unable to explain;
  - Does not get bank statements or bills;
  - Makes new or unusual gifts to family or others, such as a "new best friend";
  - Changes beneficiaries of a will, life insurance, or retirement funds; or
  - Has a caregiver, friend, or relative who suddenly begins handling her money.
- *Rose says she is afraid or seems afraid of a relative, caregiver, or friend~*
- *A relative, caregiver, friend, or someone else keeps Rose from having visitors or phone calls, does not let her speak for herself, or seems to be controlling her decisions.*

What Can You Do if Rose Has Been Exploited?

- Call the emergency 911 number if Rose is in immediate danger.
- Call local adult protective services or the police or sheriff. You may be required by law to do this.
- Alert Rose's bank or credit card company.
- Call the local prosecutor or state attorney general.
- Call the long-term care ombudsman program or the state Medicaid fraud control unit if Rose is in a nursing home or assisted living.

- Consider talking to a lawyer about protecting Rose from more exploitation or getting back money or property taken from her.

Each agency or professional has a different role, so you may need to call more than one. For more information, see Where to go for help on page 24 of this guide.

Be on Guard for Consumer Scams

As Rose's trustee, you should be alert to protect her money from consumer scams as well as financial exploitation. Criminals and con artists have many scams and change them all the time. They often seek unsuspecting people who have access to money. Learn to spot consumer scams against Rose—and against you as her trustee.

How Can You Protect Rose from Scams?

Consumer scams happen on the phone; through the mail, e-mail, or the Internet; and they occur in person, at home, or at a business. Here are some tips:

- *Help Rose put her number on the National Do Not Call Registry*. Go to www. donotcall.gov or call 1-888-382-1222.
- *Don't share numbers or passwords for Rose's accounts, credit cards, or Social Security,* unless you know whom you're dealing with and why they need the information.
- *After hearing a sales pitch, take time to compare prices*. Ask for information in writing and read it carefully.
- *Too good to be true?* Ask yourself why someone is trying so hard to give you a "great deal." If it sounds too good to be true, it probably is.
- *Watch out for deals that are only "good today" and that pressure you to act quickly.* Be suspicious if you are not given enough time to read a contract or get legal advice before signing. Also watch out if you are told that you need to pay the seller quickly, for example by wiring the money or sending it by courier.

- *Never pay up front for a promised prize.* Suspect a scam if you are required to pay fees or taxes to receive a prize or other financial windfall.
- *Watch for signs Rose already has been scammed.* For example, does she receive a lot of mail or e-mail for sweepstakes? Has she paid people you don't know, especially in other states or countries? Has she taken a lot of money out of the bank while she was with someone she recently met? Does she have a hard time explaining how she spent that money? Is she suddenly unable to pay for food, medicine, or utilities?

What Can You Do if Rose Has Been Scammed?

If you suspect a scam, get help. Contact a local, state, or federal agency, depending on the type of scam. You may also need to talk to a lawyer.

Local agencies to call are adult protective services, the long-term care ombudsman program, the police or sheriff, and the local Better Business Bureau.

State agencies to call are the office of the attorney general or another agency that deals with consumer protection.

Call a federal agency if scammers are in other states or countries. Federal agencies are the Consumer Financial Protection Bureau, the FBI, the Federal Trade Commission, or the U.S. Postal Inspection Service.

Each of these agencies and professionals has a different role so you may need to call more than one.

In: Money Management for Financial Caregivers ISBN: 978-1-63117-042-3
Editor: Olivia Crowder

Chapter 4

MANAGING SOMEONE ELSE'S MONEY: HELP FOR REPRESENTATIVE PAYEES AND VA FIDUCIARIES*

American Bar Association Commission on Law and Aging

WHY READ THIS GUIDE?

Like many people, you may never have been a representative payee or VA fiduciary before. That's why we created *Managing someone else's money: Help for representative payees and VA fiduciaries*. This guide will help you understand what you can and cannot do in your role as a *representative payee* or *VA fiduciary*. In both these roles, you are a *fiduciary*. For this guide, a fiduciary is anyone named to manage money or property for someone else. You'll find brief tips to help you avoid problems and resources for finding more information.

This guide is for family and friends serving as a representative payee or VA fiduciary, not for professionals or organizations. The guide does not give you legal advice. State laws vary, so you may have additional duties. Talk to a lawyer if you have questions about your duties.

---

* This guide was developed under contract for the Consumer Financial Protection Bureau and released October 2013.

If you want to learn about how to become a representative payee or VA fiduciary, this guide is not designed for you. You should contact the federal agency that pays the benefits.

Let's Start with a Scenario About How You Might Have Become a Representative Payee or VA Fiduciary

Your family member or friend receives Social Security or veterans benefits. For this guide, let's call him Roberto. The Social Security Administration has named you as *representative payee* for Roberto, or the Department of Veterans Affairs has named you as Roberto's *VA fiduciary.*

You now have the duty and power to manage his Social Security or Veterans Affairs benefit checks.

In this role on Roberto's behalf, the federal government gives you a lot of responsibility.

You are now a *fiduciary* with *fiduciary duties.*

What Is a Fiduciary?

Since you have been named to manage money or property for someone else, you are a *fiduciary*. The law requires you to manage Roberto's money for HIS benefit, not yours. It does not matter if you are managing a lot of money or a little. It does not matter if you are a family member or not.

The role of a fiduciary is a serious one and carries with it legal responsibilities. When you act as a fiduciary for Roberto, you have four basic duties that you must keep in mind:

1. Act only in Roberto's best interest.
2. Manage Roberto's money and property carefully.
3. Keep Roberto's money and property separate from yours.
4. Keep good records.

As a fiduciary, you must be trustworthy, honest, and act in good faith. If you do not meet these standards, you could be removed from that role. You could be investigated by the government and have to repay money. It's even possible you could go to jail. *That's why it's always important to remember: It's not your money!*

Representative Payee or VA Fiduciary Questions and Answers

What Is a Representative Payee or VA Fiduciary ?

A government agency may appoint someone to manage income benefits for a person who needs help managing those benefits.

For example, the Social Security Administration, the Office of Personnel Management, and the Railroad Retirement Administration call the person who is appointed a *representative payee.* The Department of Veterans Affairs has a similar program, but the person appointed is called a *VA fiduciary.* State agencies may have similar arrangements. Each agency may have different rules and procedures. This guide covers two of the largest agencies, Social Security and the VA, but the duties described in this guide may be helpful to other representative payees.

Since you have been appointed as Roberto's representative payee, we will call you a rep payee for short. Roberto is the beneficiary.

Once you are appointed as a rep payee or VA fiduciary, you must follow the basic fiduciary duties in this guide. Plus, you also must meet certain reporting requirements of the particular agency.

Different Types of Fiduciaries Exist

In your role as rep payee or VA fiduciary, you may act as or deal with other types of fiduciaries. These may include:

Agents under a power of attorney—someone names an agent to manage their money and property in case they are not able to do it.

Trustees under a revocable living trust—someone names them to manage money and property.

Guardians or Conservators —a court names them to manage money and property for someone who needs help.

What Money Does a Representative Payee or VA Fiduciary Manage?

You only have authority to manage the benefit checks of the agency appointing you. You have no legal authority to manage other property, financial affairs, or medical matters for Roberto. To control other matters, you must have legal authority from another source, such as through a power of attorney, trust, or court appointment.

Even if you are Roberto's agent under a power of attorney or a trust, or if you are his guardian or conservator, you don't have legal authority to manage his federal benefits checks. You still must be appointed representative payee or VA fiduciary by the agency paying the benefit.

Don't Expect Others to Know What a Rep Payee or VA Fiduciary Is or Does

They may not understand that you have been named as a rep payee or VA fiduciary. They may think you have either more authority or less authority than you really have. You may need to educate them. You could show them this guide and the letter appointing you.

FOUR BASIC DUTIES OF A FIDUCIARY

Duty 1. Act only in Roberto's Best Interest

Because you are dealing with Roberto's money, your duty is to make decisions that are best for him. This means you must ignore your own interests and needs, or the interests and needs of other people such as Roberto's relatives who are not his dependents.

To help act in Roberto's best interest, follow these guidelines:

- Avoid conflicts of interest. A conflict of interest happens if you make a decision about Roberto's money that may benefit someone else besides Roberto. As a fiduciary, you have a strict duty to avoid conflicts of interest—or even the appearance of a conflict of interest.
- Don't borrow, loan, or give Roberto's money to yourself or others~ The VA may allow gifts in certain circumstances, but be sure to check with them first.
- Don't pay yourself for your services. Only certain organizations or qualified individuals are allowed to charge a fee to serve as rep payee or VA fiduciary if the particular agency approves it.

Avoid Possible Conflicts of Interest

Sometimes people have good intentions, but do things they shouldn't. Because you are now a fiduciary, you should avoid any conflicts of interest. Here are a few examples of possible conflicts of interest

Whose Car Is It?

You used Roberto's money to buy a car. You use it to drive him to appointments, but most of the time you drive the car just for your own needs. This may be a conflict of interest.

Should You Do Business with Family?

Roberto needs repair work in his apartment. You hire your son and pay him from Roberto's money. This may be a conflict of interest, even though the work was needed. It appears that you have put your personal interest to benefit your son in conflict with Roberto's interests.

Duty 2. Manage Roberto's Money Carefully

As Roberto's fiduciary, you might pay bills or taxes, oversee bank accounts, pay for things he needs, and do other things to manage his benefits. You have a duty to manage Roberto's money very carefully. Use good judgment and common sense. As a fiduciary, you must be even more careful with Roberto's money than you might be with your own!

Follow these guidelines to help you make careful decisions:

- Make sure Roberto's day-to-day needs for food, clothing, and shelter are met first. Only then should you spend money on Roberto's medical, dental, and personal needs to improve his daily living conditions or comfort, such as:
  - Improvements in his home or apartment;
  - Recreational activities, magazine subscriptions, cable TV;
  - Educational or training expenses, if they are needed to improve Roberto's life; and
  - Car payments, if his other needs are met and Roberto needs or owns the car.

- Pay bills on time. Make sure bills are sent to you. Review bills and bank statements promptly.
- Protect unspent funds. After you pay Roberto's regular expenses, if money is left over, you must save it in a federally protected or state-insured interest-bearing account or U.S. savings bond. The interest earned always belongs to Roberto.
- Consider Roberto's dependents. If Roberto has a spouse or dependent family members, consult with the Social Security Administration or the VA about whether you can use any of his money to pay for their needs.
- Protect Roberto's money from creditors' claims. The law protects Roberto's benefits. Creditors are not allowed to legally take his Social Security or VA funds. If Roberto has funds from other sources (for example, pensions, gifts, savings), don't mix them with his Social Security or VA funds. Mixing funds may make it harder to protect Roberto's Social Security and VA funds from people who may have claims against him.
- Don't overlook taxes. Be aware that some people who get Social Security or other federal benefits may have to pay federal income tax, depending on their total income. As Roberto's fiduciary, each year you will receive a form showing the amount of benefits paid to him during the previous year. Consult an income tax preparer to determine whether Roberto will owe taxes. Be sure to pay taxes on time.

Can Roberto Get Any Benefits?

Find out if Roberto is eligible for other benefits that would enable his Social Security or Veterans benefit to go further.

For instance, you could help Roberto apply for other private benefits such as employer pensions or disability, or public benefits such as Medicaid, housing assistance, or food stamps (now known as Supplemental Nutrition Assistance Program, or SNAP). Use the National Council on Aging benefits check-up at www.BenefitsCheckUp.org.

The Area Agency on Aging where Roberto lives can help you find information. Find the local Area Agency on Aging through the Eldercare Locator at www.eldercare.gov.

Medicaid Is Complicated

Get legal advice and be very careful about decisions that may affect Roberto's eligibility for Medicaid. The Medicaid program provides medical assistance and long-term care to low-income people. It may have another name in your state. To find your state Medicaid agency, visit: www.benefits.gov/benefits/browse-by-category/category/MED.

Duty 3. Keep Roberto's Money Separate

Never mix Roberto's benefit money with your own or someone else's. Mixing money makes it unclear who owns what. Confused records can get you in trouble with government agencies and law enforcement.

Follow these guidelines:

- Separate means separate. Never deposit Roberto's money into your own or someone else's bank account or investment account. The VA fiduciary program makes an exception to this rule if you are a fiduciary for your spouse.
- Avoid joint accounts. If you and Roberto already have benefit money in a joint account, take his money out and put it in a new account. The box to the right shows you how to title the account and sign checks. Arrange for direct deposit of his benefits.
- Pay Roberto's expenses from his funds, not yours. Spending your money and then paying yourself back makes it hard to keep good records. If you really need to use your money, keep receipts for the expense and maintain a good record of why, what, and when you paid yourself.
- Don't sign contracts or leases on Roberto's behalf, even if they are entirely paid by benefits. You don't have the authority to sign contracts or leases for Roberto, unless you have some other legal arrangement such as a power of attorney or guardianship.

How to Title an Account

If you are a rep payee	
For bank accounts	(Name of beneficiary) by (Your name), representative payee OR (Your name), representative payee for (Name of beneficiary)
For U.S. savings bonds	(Name of beneficiary) (His Social Security Number), for whom (Your name) is representative payee for Social Security benefits

If you are a VA fiduciary	
For bank accounts	(Name of beneficiary) by (Your name), fiduciary OR (Your name), fiduciary for (Name of beneficiary)
For U.S. savings bonds	(Name of beneficiary) (His Social Security Number), under custodianship by designation of the Department of Veterans Affairs of the Department of Veterans Affairs

DUTY 4. KEEP GOOD RECORDS AND REPORT AS REQUIRED

You must keep true and complete records of Roberto's money and how it is used. As Roberto's fiduciary, you must be able to account for everything you've done with his money.

Practice good recordkeeping habits:

- Keep a detailed list of all money you receive or spend for Roberto. Your records should include the amount of checks written or deposited, dates, reasons, names of people or companies involved, interest rates on savings or investments, and other important information.
- Keep receipts and notes, even for small expenses. For example, write, "$50, groceries, ABC Grocery Store, May 2" on the receipt soon after you spend the money.

- Avoid paying in cash. Try not to pay Roberto's expenses with cash. Also, try not to use an ATM card to withdraw cash or write checks to cash. If you need to use cash, be sure to keep receipts or notes.
- Make annual reports on time:
  - ú If you are a Social Security representative payee, every year you must fill out a form to account for the benefits you have received and spent and verify your status and the beneficiary's. You can fill this form out online at: www.socialsecurity.gov/payee.
  - If you are a VA fiduciary, you must submit accountings when you are asked for them. For the VA form, go to: www.vba.va.gov/pubs/forms/VBA-21p4706b-ARE.pdf.
- Keep the agency informed about Roberto. You must notify the agency of any event or change in Roberto's situation that will affect the amount of his benefits or how they are received. For example, let the agency know if Roberto:
  - Moves or changes his contact information
  - Has a change in income from any sources
  - Is imprisoned or faces criminal charges for a felony
  - Has a change in dependents
  - Will be outside of the U.S. for 30 days or more ú Improves to the point that he no longer needs a rep payee or fiduciary, or no longer qualifies for benefits
  - Dies
- If you are a representative payee and Roberto receives Supplemental Security Income (SSI), you have special reporting requirements. Let the Social Security Administration know if Roberto:
  - Moves to or from a hospital, nursing home, correctional facility, or other institution
  - Separates from his spouse or begins again living with his spouse after they were separated
  - Moves into someone else's household or someone moves into or out of his household
- Special reporting for VA fiduciaries. Let the VA know if Roberto is receiving hospital treatment or other institutional, nursing, or residential care.
- Keep the agency informed about yourself. Let the agency know if you:
  - Move

- No longer wish to be Roberto's payee
- Are convicted of a felony or face criminal charges for a felony
- Have any other change of circumstances that would affect your performance as a payee

MORE THINGS YOU SHOULD KNOW

What if There Are Other Fiduciaries?

Other fiduciaries may have some authority to make decisions for Roberto. For example, Roberto may have an agent under a power of attorney who is managing other money or property for him. The court might have appointed a guardian of property, or there may be a trustee under a trust account. Remember, you only have authority over Roberto's VA, Social Security, or other federal benefit.

To the extent that you can, if you coordinate with Roberto's other fiduciaries, you will generally be able to manage his affairs more cost effectively.

How Can You Avoid Problems with Family or Friends?

Family or friends may not agree with your decisions about Roberto's money. To help reduce any friction, follow the four duties and the guidelines we've given you.

Sharing information may help. For example, you might want to share reports you complete or summaries of how you've spent Roberto's money, unless Roberto has said that you should not. It usually is easier to deal with questions about a decision when it happens than to deal with suspicion and anger that may build over a long time. In the end, you have to make the final decisions.

Some family or friends may be so difficult that it is better not to share information with them. Use your best judgment.

If family or friends don't agree with your decisions, try to get someone to help sort it out—for example, a family counselor or mediator. See *Where to go for help* on page 22 of this guide.

WATCH OUT FOR FINANCIAL EXPLOITATION

Family, friends, neighbors, caregivers, fiduciaries, business people, and others may try to take advantage of Roberto. They may take his money without permission, fail to repay money they owe, charge him too much for services, or just not do things he has paid them to do. These may be examples of financial exploitation or financial abuse. As Roberto's rep payee or VA fiduciary you should help protect him. You should know the signs of financial exploitation for five important reasons:

1. Roberto may still control some of his funds and could be exploited;
2. Even if Roberto does not control any of his funds, he still may be exploited;
3. Roberto may have been exploited already, and you may still be able to do something about that;
4. People may try to take advantage of you as Roberto's rep payee or VA fiduciary; and
5. Knowing what to look for will help you avoid doing things you should not do, protecting you from claims that you have exploited Roberto.

Look for These Common Signs of Financial Exploitation

- You think that some money or property is missing.
- Roberto says that some money or property is missing.
- You notice sudden changes in Roberto's spending or savings. For example, he:
  - Takes out lots of money from the bank without explanation;
  - Tries to wire large amounts of money;
  - Uses the ATM a lot;
  - Is not able to pay bills that are usually paid;
  - Buys things or services that don't seem necessary;
  - Puts names on bank or other accounts that you do not recognize or that he is unwilling or unable to explain;
  - Does not get bank statements or bills;
  - Makes new or unusual gifts to family or others, such as a "new best friend";

- Changes beneficiaries of a will, life insurance, or retirement funds; or
- Has a caregiver, friend, or relative who suddenly begins handling his money.

- Roberto says he is afraid or seems afraid of a relative, caregiver, or friend.
- A relative, caregiver, friend, or someone else keeps Roberto from having visitors or phone calls, or does not let him speak for himself, or seems to be controlling his decisions~

What Can You Do if Roberto Has Been Exploited?

- Call the emergency 911 number if Roberto is in immediate danger.
- Call local adult protective services or the police or sheriff. You may be required by law to do this.
- Alert Roberto's bank or credit card company.
- Call the local prosecutor or state attorney general.
- Call the long-term care ombudsman program or the state Medicaid fraud control unit if Roberto is in a nursing home or assisted living.
- Consider talking to a lawyer about protecting Roberto from more exploitation or getting back money or property taken from him.

Each agency or professional has a different role, so you may need to call more than one. For more information, see *Where to go for help* on page 22 of this guide.

Be on Guard for Consumer Scams

As Roberto's fiduciary, you should be alert to protect his money from consumer scams as well as financial exploitation. Criminals and con artists have many scams, and change them all the time. They often seek unsuspecting people who have access to money. Learn to spot consumer scams against Roberto—and against you as his fiduciary.

How Can You Protect Roberto from Scams?

Consumer scams happen on the phone; through the mail, e-mail, or the Internet; and they occur in person, at home, or at a business.

Here are some tips:

- Help Roberto put his number on the National Do Not Call Registry. Go to www. donotcall.gov or call 1-888-382-1222.
- Don't share numbers or passwords for Roberto's accounts, credit cards, or Social Security, unless you know whom you're dealing with and why they need the information.
- After hearing a sales pitch, take time to compare prices. Ask for information in writing and read it carefully.
- Too good to be true? Ask yourself why someone is trying so hard to give you a "great deal." If it sounds too good to be true, it probably is.
- Watch out for deals that are only "good today" and that pressure you to act quickly. Be suspicious if you are not given enough time to read a contract or get legal advice before signing. Also watch out if you are told that you need to pay the seller quickly, for example by wiring the money or sending it by courier.
- Never pay up front for a promised prize. Suspect a scam if you are required to pay fees or taxes to receive a prize or other financial windfall.
- Watch for signs Roberto already has been scammed. For example, does he receive a lot of mail or e-mail for sweepstakes? Has he paid people you don't know, especially in other states or countries? Has he taken a lot of money out of the bank while he was with someone he recently met? Does he have a hard time explaining how he spent that money? Is he suddenly unable to pay for food, medicine, or utilities?

What Can You Do if Roberto Has Been Scammed?

If you suspect a scam, get help. Contact a local, state, or federal agency, depending on the type of scam. You may also need to talk to a lawyer.

Local agencies to call are adult protective services, the long-term care ombudsman program, the police or sheriff, and the local Better Business Bureau.

State agencies to call are the office of the attorney general or another agency that deals with consumer protection.

Call a federal agency if scammers are in other states or countries. Federal agencies are the Consumer Financial Protection Bureau, the FBI, the Federal Trade Commission, or the U.S. Postal Inspection Service.

Each of these agencies and professionals has a different role so you may need to call more than one.

For more information, see Where to go for help.

Common Consumer Scams	
Relative in need	Someone who pretends to be a family member or friend calls or e-mails you to say they are in trouble and need you to wire money right away.
Charity appeals	You get a call or letter from someone asking for money for a fake charity—either the charity does not exist or the charity did not call or write to you.
Lottery or sweepstakes	You get a call or e-mail that you have a chance to win a lot of money through a foreign country's sweepstakes or lottery. The caller will offer tips about how to win if you pay a fee or buy something. Or the caller or e-mail says you already have won and you must give your bank account information or pay a fee to collect your winnings.
Home improvement	Scammers take money for repairs and then they never return to do the work or they do bad work. Sometimes they break something to create more work or they say that things need work when they don't.
Free lunch	Scammers invite you to a free lunch and seminar, and then pressure you to give them information about your money, and to invest the money with them. They offer you "tips" or "guaranteed returns."
Free trip	Scammers say you've won a free trip but they ask for a credit card number or advance cash to hold the reservation.
Government money	You get a call or letter that seems to be from a government agency. Scammers say that if you give a credit card number or send a money order, you can apply for government help with housing, home repairs, utilities, or taxes.
Drug plans	Scammers pretend they are with Medicare prescription drug plans, and try to sell Medicare discount drug cards that are not valid. Companies with Medicare drug plans are not allowed to send unsolicited mail, emails, or phone calls.
Identity theft	Scammers steal personal information—such as a name, date of birth, Social Security number, account number, and mother's maiden name— and use the information to open credit cards or get a mortgage in someone else's name.

Fake "official" mail	Scammers send letters or e-mails that look like they are from a legitimate bank, business, or agency to try to get your personal information or bank account number.

WHERE TO GO FOR HELP

Local and State Agencies

Adult Protective Services

Find the state or local agencies that receive and investigate reports of suspected elder or adult abuse, neglect, or exploitation by contacting the national Eldercare Locator.

1-800-677-1116

www.eldercare.gov

Area Agency on Aging/Aging and Disability Resource Center

Find the local agencies that can give you information about aging and disability services and whether there are any support groups for fiduciaries or caregivers by contacting the national Eldercare Locator.

1-800-677-1116

www.eldercare.gov

Attorney General

Find a listing of state attorneys general on the website of the National Association of Attorneys General. Attorneys general can take action against consumer fraud.

www.naag.org

Better Business Bureau

Find a state or local bureau on the website of the national Better Business Bureau. The BBB can help consumers with complaints against businesses.

www.bbb.org

Long-Term Care Ombudsman Program

Find state and local advocates for residents of long-term care facilities by contacting the national Eldercare Locator.

1-800-677-1116

www.eldercare.gov

Mediators

Find a listing of local mediators on the website of the national Association for Conflict Resolution. Mediation can help resolve disputes and may sometimes be an alternative to legal action.

www.acrnet.org (Click on "Membership," then "Membership Directory," then "Search")

Medicaid/Medical Assistance

Find a listing of state agencies that provide Medicaid/Medical Assistance on the federal Benefits.gov website.

www.benefits.gov/benefits/browse-bycategory/category/MED

Medicaid Fraud Control Unit

Find a listing of state units on the website of the National Association of Medicaid Fraud Control Units. These units investigate and prosecute abuse and fraud by health care providers.

www.namfcu.net

Police or Sheriff

Find a law enforcement agency by checking the local directory.

Federal Agencies

Numerous federal agencies play a role in combating fraud and abuse and educating consumers. Contact them for more information.

Consumer Financial Protection Bureau

1-855-411-CFPB

www.consumerfinance.gov

Do Not Call Registry

1-888-382-1222 www.donotcall.gov

Federal Bureau of Investigation

www.fbi.gov/scams-safety

Federal Trade Commission

1-877-FTC-HELP (382-4357)

www.consumer.ftc.gov

Financial Fraud Enforcement Task Force

www.stopfraud.gov

Postal Inspection Service

1-877-876-2455

www.postalinspectors.uspis.gov

Social Security Administration

1-800-772-1213

www.socialsecurity.gov/payee

Department of Veterans Affairs

1-888-407-0144

www.benefits.va.gov/fiduciary

For Legal Help

Free Legal Services for People Over Age 60

Find local programs that provide free legal help to people over age 60 by contacting the national Eldercare Locator.

1-800-677-1116

www.eldercare.gov

Free Legal Services for Low-Income People

Find local programs that provide free legal help to low-income people on the website of the Legal Services Corporation.

www.lsc.gov/find-legal-aid

Fee-for-Service Lawyers

This is a web page sponsored by the American Bar Association. It provides information about how to find a lawyer in each state. It also has information about legal resources available in each state, how to check whether a lawyer is licensed, and what to do if you have problems with a lawyer.

www.findlegalhelp.org

For Accounting Help

Accountants

Find a local certified public accountant on the website of the American Institute of CPAs.

www.aicpa.org/ForThePublic/FindACPA/Pages/ FindACPA.aspx

In: Money Management for Financial Caregivers ISBN: 978-1-63117-042-3
Editor: Olivia Crowder

Chapter 5

INVESTOR BULLETIN: TOP TIPS FOR SELECTING A FINANCIAL PROFESSIONAL*

Securities and Exchange Commission, Office of Investor Education and Advocacy

Choosing a financial professional-whether a stockbroker, a financial planner, or an investment adviser-is an important decision. Consider the tips below as you make your choice. Also the third page of this document has a list of questions you can ask a financial professional whose services you are considering.

TIP 1. DO YOUR HOMEWORK AND ASK QUESTIONS

A lot of the information you'll need to make a choice will be in the documents the financial professional can provide you about opening an account or starting a relationship.

---

* This bulletin was released by the Securities and Exchange Commission, September 2012.

You should read them carefully. If you don't understand something, ask questions until you do. It's your money and you should feel comfortable asking about it.

Tip 2. Find out Whether the Products and Services Available Are Right for You

Financial professionals offer a range of financial and investment services such as:

- Financial planning
- Ongoing money management
- Advice on choosing securities
- Tax and retirement planning
- Insurance advice

Just like a grocery store offers more products than a convenience store, some financial professionals offer a wide range of products or services, while others offer a more limited selection.

Think about what you might need, and ask about what would be available to you. For example, do you want or need:

- Access to a broad range of securities, such as stocks, options and bonds, or will you mostly want a few types such as mutual funds, exchange traded funds, or insurance products?
- A one-time review or financial plan?
- To do your own research, but use the financial professional to make your trades or to provide a second opinion occasionally?
- A recommendation each time you think about changing or making an investment?
- Ongoing investment management, with the financial professional getting your permission before any purchase or sale is made?
- Ongoing investment management, where the financial professional decides what purchases or sales are made, and you are told about it afterwards?

Tip 3. Understand How You'll Pay for Services and Products, and How Your Financial Professional Gets Paid as Well

Many firms offer more than one type of account. You may be able to pay for services differently depending on the type of account you choose. For example, you might pay:

- An hourly fee for advisory services;
- A flat fee, such as $500 per year, for an annual portfolio review or $2,000 for a financial plan;
- A commission on the securities bought or sold, such as $12 per trade;
- A fee (sometimes called a "load") based on the amount you invest in a mutual fund or variable annuity
- A "mark-up" when you buy "house" products (such as bonds that the broker holds in inventory), or a "mark-down" when you sell them

Depending on what services you want, one type of account may cost you less than another. Ask about what alternatives make sense for you.

And remember: even if you don't pay the financial professional directly, such as through an annual fee, that person is still getting paid. For example, someone else may be paying the financial professional for selling specific products. However, those payments may be built into the costs you ultimately pay, such as the expenses associated with buying or holding a financial product.

While some of these fees may seem small, it is important to keep in mind that they can add up, and in the end take away from the profits you otherwise could be making from your investments.

Tip 4. Ask About the Financial Professional's Experience and Credentials

Financial professionals hold different licenses. For example, financial professionals who are broker-dealers must take an exam to hold a license, while state regulators often require investment advisers to hold certain licenses. Financial professionals also have a wide range of educational and professional backgrounds. They may also have certain designations after their names, which are titles given by industry groups that themselves are not regulated or subject to standards other than their own.

If a financial professional has an industry designation, like "CFA," you can look up what it stands for at the "Understanding Investment Professional Designations" page on FINRA's website at www.finra.org. Don't accept a professional designation as a badge of knowledge without knowing what it means.

Tip 5. Ask the Financial Professional if He or She Has Had a Disciplinary History with a Government Regulator or Had Customer Complaints

Even if a close friend or relative has recommended a financial professional, you should check the person's background for signs of any potential problems, such as a disciplinary history by a regulator or customer complaints.

The SEC, FINRA, and state securities regulators keep records on the disciplinary history of many of the financial professionals they regulate.

Check the background of your financial professional to learn more or to help confirm what he or she has told you:

- For financial professionals who are brokers: you can find background information on the person and his/her firm at FINRA's BrokerCheck website.
- For financial professionals who are investment advisers registered with the SEC: you can find background information on the person and his/ her firm at the SEC's Investment Adviser Public Disclosure database.
- State securities regulators also have background information on brokers as well as certain investment advisers. You can find your state regulator at www.nasaa.org.

INVESTOR CHECKLIST
SOME KEY QUESTIONS FOR HIRING A FINANCIAL PROFESSIONAL

Expectations of the Relationship

- ü How often should I expect to hear from you?
- How often will you review my account or make recommendations to me?
- If my investments aren't doing well, will you call me and recommend something else?
- If I invest with you, how can I keep track of how well my investments are doing?
- Experience and Background
- What experience do you have, especially with people like me? What percentage of your time would you estimate that you spend on people with situations and goals that are similar to mine?
- What education have you had that relates to your work?
- What professional licenses do you hold?
- Are you registered with the SEC, a state securities regulator, or FINRA?
- How long have you done this type of work?
- Have you ever been disciplined by a regulator? If yes, what was the problem and how was it resolved?
- Have you had customer complaints? If yes, how many, what were they about, and how were they resolved?

Products

- What type of products do you offer? ü How many different products do you offer?
- Do you offer "house" products? If so, what types of products are they, and do you receive any incentives for selling these products, or for maintaining them in a customer's account? What kind of incentives are they?

Payments and Fees

- Given my situation and what I'm looking for, what is the [best / most cost effective] way for me to pay for financial services? Why?
- What are the fees that I will pay for products and services?
- How and when will I see the fees I pay?
- Which of those fees will I pay directly (such as a commission on a stock trade) and which are taken directly from the products I own (such as some mutual fund expenses)
- How do you get paid?
- If I invested $1000 with you today, approximately how much would you get paid during the following year, based on my investment?
- Does someone else (such as a fund company) pay you for offering or selling these products or services?

RELATED INFORMATION

For additional educational information, see the SEC's website for individual investors, Investor.gov. For additional information about selecting a financial professional, see:

SEC Fast Answers: "Financial Planners," "Investment Advisers"
SEC Publication: "Investment Advisers: What You Need to Know Before Choosing One"
SEC Publication: "Protect Your Money: Check out Brokers and Investment Advisers"
FINRA Publication: "Selecting Investment Professionals"
National Association of Personal Financial Advisers Publication: "Pursuit of a Financial Adviser: Field Guide"

You may also be interested in:

FINRA Mutual Fund Fee Calculator
Information about different types of financial products is available at http://www.investor. gov/investing-basics/investment-products

The Office of Investor Education and Advocacy has provided this information as a service to investors. It is neither a legal interpretation nor a statement of SEC policy. If you have questions concerning the meaning or application of a particular law or rule, please consult with an attorney who specializes in securities law.

In: Money Management for Financial Caregivers ISBN: 978-1-63117-042-3
Editor: Olivia Crowder

Chapter 6

INVESTMENT ADVISERS: WHAT YOU NEED TO KNOW BEFORE CHOOSING ONE*

Securities and Exchange Commission, Office of Investor Education and Advocacy

The Securities and Exchange Commission (SEC) receives many questions about investment advisers—what they are and how to go about choosing one. This document answers some of the typical questions we receive from investors about investment advisers. This Q&A is for the benefit of investors. You should not rely on it to determine if you need to register as an investment adviser.

Q: What is an investment adviser?

A: An investment adviser is an individual or a firm that is in the business of giving advice about securities to clients. For instance, individuals or firms that receive compensation for giving advice on investing in stocks, bonds, mutual funds, or exchange traded funds are investment advisers. Some investment advisers manage portfolios of securities.

---

* This is an edited, reformatted and augmented version of a Securities and Exchange Commission, Office of Investor Education and Advocacy publication, originally posted on the following website: http://www.sec.gov/investor/pubs/invadvisers.htm) dated August 7, 2012.

Q: What is the difference between an investment adviser and a financial planner?

A: Most financial planners are investment advisers, but not all investment advisers are financial planners. Some financial planners assess every aspect of your financial life—including saving, investments, insurance, taxes, retirement, and estate planning—and help you develop a detailed strategy or financial plan for meeting all your financial goals.

Others call themselves financial planners, but they may only be able to recommend that you invest in a narrow range of products, and sometimes products that aren't securities.

Before you hire any financial professional, you should know exactly what services you need, what services the professional can deliver, any limitations on what they can recommend, what services you're paying for, how much those services cost, and how the adviser or planner gets paid.

Q: What questions should I ask when choosing an investment adviser or financial planner?

A: Here are some of the questions you should always ask when hiring any financial professional:

- What experience do you have, especially with people in my circumstances?
- Where did you go to school? What is your recent employment history?
- What licenses do you hold? Are you registered with the SEC, a state, or the Financial Industry Regulatory Authority (FINRA)?
- What products and services do you offer?
- Can you only recommend a limited number of products or services to me? If so, why?
- How are you paid for your services? What is your usual hourly rate, flat fee, or commission?
- Have you ever been disciplined by any government regulator for unethical or improper conduct or been sued by a client who was not happy with the work you did?
- For registered investment advisers, will you send me a copy of both parts of your Form ADV?

Be sure to meet potential advisers "face to face" to make sure you get along. And remember: there are many types of individuals who can help you develop a personal financial plan and manage your hard–earned money. The most important thing is that you know your financial goals, have a plan in place, and check out the professional you chose with your securities regulator.

Q: How do investment advisers get paid?

A: Before you hire any financial professional—whether it's a stockbroker, a financial planner, or an investment adviser—you should always find out and make sure you understand how that person gets paid. Investment advisers generally are paid in any of the following ways:

- A percentage of the value of the assets they manage for you;
- An hourly fee for the time they spend working for you;
- A fixed fee;
- A commission on the securities they sell (if the adviser is also a broker-dealer); or
- Some combination of the above.

Each compensation method has potential benefits and possible drawbacks, depending on your individual needs. Ask the investment advisers you interview to explain the differences to you before you do business with them, and get several opinions before making your decision. Also ask if the fee is negotiable.

Q: Do investment advisers have to register with the SEC?

A: Depending on their size, investment advisers have to register with either the SEC or the state securities agency where they have their principal place of business. For the most part, investment advisers who manage $100 million or more in client assets must register with the SEC. If they manage less than $100 million, they must register with the state securities agency in the state where they have their principal place of business.

Q: How do I find out whether an investment adviser ever had problems with a government regulator or has a disciplinary history?

A: Most investment advisers must fill out a form called "Form ADV." They must file their Form ADVs with either the SEC or the state securities agency in the state where they have their principal place of business, depending on the amount of assets they manage.

Form ADV consists of two parts. Part 1 contains information about the adviser's business and whether they've had problems with regulators or clients. Part 2 outlines the adviser's services, fees, and strategies. Before you hire someone to be your investment adviser, always ask for, and carefully read, both parts of Form ADV.

You can get copies of Form ADV by accessing the Investment Adviser Public Disclosure (IAPD) website at http://www.adviserinfo.sec.gov/.

You can also get copies of Form ADV from the investment adviser, your state securities regulator or the SEC, depending on the size of the adviser. You can find out how to get in touch with your state securities regulator through the North American Securities Administrators Association, Inc.'s (NASAA) website or by calling (202) 737-0900. Ask your state securities regulator whether they've had any complaints about the adviser, and ask them to check the CRD (Central Registration Depository).

If the SEC registers the investment adviser, you can get a copy of the Form ADV by accessing How to Request Public Documents. In addition, at the SEC's headquarters, you can visit our Public Reference Room from 10:00 a.m. to 3:00 p.m. to obtain copies of SEC records and documents.

Q: What should I do if the financial professional claims that he or she is "certified"?

A: If the professional you're considering claims to be a CFP® certificant, you should also visit the website of the Certified Financial Planner Board of Standards, Inc. (CFB Board) to see if the professional is, in fact, certified as a CFP® professional and whether the professional's certification has been suspended or revoked by the CFP Board. You can also call the CFP Board at (888) 237-6275 to obtain other disciplinary information about the professional.

Q: Are investment advisers required to have credentials?

A: While some investment advisers and financial planners have credentials -- such as CFP® certification or CFA (chartered financial analyst) -- no state or federal law requires these credentials. Many states require advisers to pass a proficiency exam or meet other requirements.

Investment advisers and financial planners may come from many different educational and professional backgrounds. Before you hire a financial professional, be sure to ask about their background. If they have a credential, ask them what it means and what they had to do to earn it. Also, find out what organization issued the credential, and then contact the organization to verify whether the professional you're considering did, in fact, earn the credential and whether the professional remains in good standing with the organization. For information on various financial professional credentials and the entities that issue them, please visit FINRA's website and read Understanding Financial Professional Designations.

CONCLUSION

For more information about choosing investment advisers see:

Get the Facts: The SEC's Roadmap to Saving and Investing (http://www. sec.gov/ investor/pubs/roadmap.htm),

Invest Wisely: Advice from your Securities Regulators (http://www. sec. gov/investor/pubs/inws.htm) and

Ask Questions (http://www.sec.gov/investor/pubs/askquestions.htm).

INDEX

A

B

C

D

E

F

G

H

I

L

M